Haute-Savoie

PATHMASTER GUIDES

CIRCULAR 30 WALKS FROM REGIONAL CENTRES

HAUTE SAVOIE

Norman Buckley

Series Editor
Richard Sale

The Crowood Press

First published in 1990 by
The Crowood Press Ltd
Gipsy Lane
Swindon
SN2 6DQ

British Library Cataloguing in Publication Data
Buckley, Norman
    Haute Savoie – (Pathmaster guide series)
    1. France. Burgandy. – Visitors' guides
    I. Title   II. Series
    914.44904839
    ISBN 1 85223 422 9

Picture Credits
Black and white photographs throughout, and cover photographs by the author; all maps by Malcolm Walker.

Acknowledgements
I would like to take this opportunity to express my grateful thanks to the French Government Tourist Office in London and many local tourist offices throughout Haute-Savoie for a wealth of useful information, and also to my wife, June, whose enthusiastic support greatly facilitated the necessary fieldwork.

In places times from timetables and certain costs, including fares, have been quoted. These were correct at time of going to press, but it cannot be guaranteed that they will remain the same in subsequent years.

Typeset by Carreg Limited, Nailsea, Bristol
Printed in Great Britain by Redwood Press Ltd, Melksham, Wilts

CONTENTS

Preface   6

Introduction   9

The Area   33

The Walks
  Annecy   50
  Chamonix   77
  Morzine/Samoëns/Taninges   109
  Thonon/Evian/Abondance   127

Appendices
  I   Tour de Mont Blanc   151
  II Chamonix – The Natural Environment   153
  III Vocabulary   155

PREFACE

Since man first learned to stand on two legs, walking has been the essential means of personal movement, although this has gradually diminished over the last few centuries as more and more sophisticated mechanical aids have been invented. Walking simply for pleasure is a comparatively recent development, the pleasure being clearly subjective and varying greatly from individual to individual. It derives essentially from the combination of a feeling of well-being resulting from the physical exercise, enjoyment of the beauty or interest of the surroundings, and a sense of achievement, which for many reaches its ultimate in walks which include the ascent of a mountain peak.

The balance of these elements will influence the walker's choice of routes. To the 'peak-bagger', the achievement is all, and a shortish walk along a canal tow-path or river bank will offer little satisfaction. To another type of walker the considerable physical effort required for a mountain ascent, or the fright of steep and possibly dangerous places will completely spoil an otherwise enjoyable walk.

There is also another dimension to walking, best illustrated by nineteenth-century German romanticism, whereby the freedom of physical movement – wandering – is matched by the consequent freedom of the spirit. Where and how far the wanderer travels, and whether or not there is a destination, is immaterial; what is important is the freedom to roam at will, which becomes the end in itself. The first song of Schubert's *Die Schöne Mullerin* song-cycle and Mahler's '*Lieder eines fahrenden Gesellen*' are musical examples of the expression of the joy of wandering. Whilst the use of a footpath guide such as this would appear to be a contradiction of the freedom to wander at will, I do believe that all true walkers experience from time to time the same uplift of the spirit, which contributes in no small measure to their overall enjoyment.

My own taste in walking is fairly catholic. I freely admit to a particular love of mountains and in this regard Haute-Savoie is a superb choice. Haute-Savoie – the very name conjures up visions of high Alpine mountains, rugged, inaccessible crags, and another world of permanent ice and snow. These are absolutely accurate visions of a region including the highest mountain in Europe. These high places are not for the walker, except to be gazed at in wonder and admiration as he or she follows more accessible routes, yet Haute-Savoie is not all mountainous. There are plenty of valleys, rivers and forests to please all tastes.

The philosophy of this book is that most visitors to Haute-Savoie will wish to embrace a range of holiday activity, combining visits to old and attractive towns, châteaux, abbeys and the like, possibly with sporting activities, and certainly with at least some walking on footpaths. However, my experience has shown me that without a guide the latter can be quite frustrating and difficult to achieve on the Continent. Time and time again I have found that although an area of countryside appears to be suitable for walking and footpaths, with or without signposts, can be seen leading up a hillside or into a forest, there is too much uncertainty to be able to set off with any degree of confidence. Will the path continue or will it fade away? Does it lead to any objective? Is there a right of way or will there be obstructions? Does it climb very high? Will it be entirely safe for adults or young children? Is there a different return route possible? What do the instructions on a board really mean; are there phrases for which my translation is not adequate?

This guide has been written in order to remove all these uncertainties and in each walk the significant features are described in such a way that prospective walkers will be able to select in advance whatever kind of walk appeals.

The thirty walks cover a wide spectrum, from river valley to mountain peak. Many are given with route variations which add to the overall flexibility of choice.

I can only hope that those following in my footsteps enjoy walking in Haute-Savoie as much as I have done. From my acquaintance with a fair amount of Europe, I honestly cannot think of anywhere where I would prefer to walk ... and I had to do it without the considerable advantage of a Pathmaster guide!

Norman A. Buckley

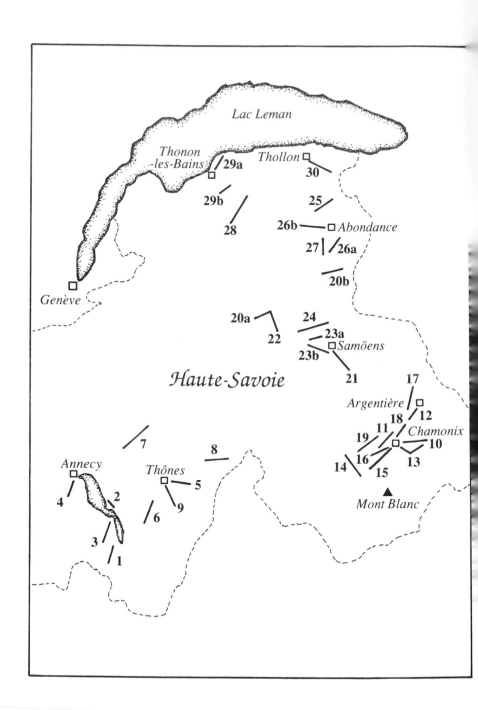

Lac Leman

Thonon
-les-Bains /29a Thollon
30

29b 25/

28 26b ⎯⎯⎯ Abondance

27 | /26a

20b

Genève

20a 24
22 23a
Samöens
23b

21

Haute-Savoie

17
Argentière
18 /12
11 Chamonix
19 10
7 16 13
8 14 15
Annecy Thônes 5
4 2 9
6 Mont Blanc
3
1

INTRODUCTION

Walking in France

For a variety of good and well-established reasons, France has long been esteemed as a place for holidays. High on the list of reasons must come the climate, the food and drink, the winter sports, the variety of scenery, the beaches, the uncrowded roads, and, perhaps, the benefits of duty-free shopping in cross-Channel hypermarkets. Walking, it must be said, has in the past hardly featured among these considerations. However, I am sure that this situation must change. France is a large and beautiful country with mountains, rolling hills and gentle countryside in profusion; it has huge areas of territory immensely attractive to walkers, and an overall population density only about half that of the UK. Tourism is regarded as important, and much attention is given to the various facilities which are likely to attract visitors. This applies at all levels, from central government down to the smallest community, and the way in which the approach roads to quite modest towns are decorated with signs proclaiming the local attractions is clear evidence of this. Equally evident is the expenditure on sporting facilities, accommodation of all kinds, tourist offices, and publicity material. Most towns and large villages with any pretension to good countryside have recognised that footpaths for recreational walking could well be important, and have set about the necessary organisation and advertising. In some cases the actual paths have been improved, steps and handrails provided as required, and undergrowth cleared. More frequently, signposts and waymarking with paint in a variety of colours and shapes are to be found. Inevitably, not all the waymarking is easy to follow; signs at crucial points may be missing and in some cases (Walk 4 in this book being a good example) an area has so many organised routes with their various colour codes that the walker is spending more time looking at paint marks on trees than at the scenery. The description of a walk in such an area becomes almost tiresome in the necessary fullness of detail.

The tourist offices, some of which still carry the traditional title of *Syndicat d'Initiative*, are usually willing and able to provide information on footpaths within their own particular areas. Haute-Savoie, being prime walking country, is generally well provided with signposted footpaths and the great majority of the walks described in this book use one or more such paths.

Another development in France, as in the UK, is the continuous long-distance footpath, most of which are called *Grandes Randonnées* and given an identification number. GR5 and GR96 pass through Haute-Savoie, GR5 being an international route connecting the Netherlands with the French Mediterranean coast. Other long-distance paths have a theme appropriate to the particular area; the following feature in the walks selected for this book: *Sentier du Léman littoral* (LL) – following close to the south shore of Lac Léman; *Balcon du Léman* (BL) – a few miles further south, generally on higher ground; *Sentier des Portes du Soleil* (PS) – runs East/West across northern Haute-Savoie; *Tour du Mont Blanc* (TMB) – a celebrated circuit of Europe's highest mountain; *Tour du Lac d'Annecy* (TLA) – a circuit of the beautiful Annecy lake; *Grande Traversée Alpes* (GTA) – enters Haute-Savoie to the south of Annecy and heads generally north towards Bonneville; *Sentier du pays de Mont Blanc* (SPMB) – to the north and west of Mont Blanc.

Several of these footpaths have 'variant' sections which follow alternative routes. It has to be said that the signposting of these footpaths does not always match their apparent importance and, in at least one instance, the path does not exist where shown on the IGN map. Should a footpath be lost for any reason, use the same commonsense approach to farming activity as you would in the UK. Do not trample through growing crops and keep to the field edges wherever possible. Avoid unnecessary disturbance of farm animals and, above all, be friendly and polite to local farmers and farm workers, who will probably be willing and able to help you regain a a lost route. There is a *Code du Randonneur* which is very similar to our Country Code:-

Love and respect nature.
Avoid unnecessary noise.
Do not leave litter.
Do not pick flowers or dig up plants.
Do not disturb wildlife.
Re-close all gates.
Protect and preserve the habitat.
Do not smoke or light fires in forests.
Keep to the footpath.
Respect and understand country people and their way of life.
Think of others as well as yourself.

Experienced walkers will hardly need to study this code, as its requirements will be followed by second nature.

Other good advice is to check the local weather forecast before setting out on an ambitious, particularly a mountain, walk, and also to leave a note of destination and likely route at the hotel or hostel. It is generally considered that walking alone is less safe than having two or more in the party. Whilst this cannot be disputed, there are many (most notably A. Wainwright) who argue that solo walking is much to be preferred. You have only yourself to please and destination, route, speed and refreshment are entirely your own choice.

The following 'advice to hikers' is given by the Chamonix mountain footpath working team:

Be prudent!
1.   Rambling in the mountains requires a good moral and physical preparation. Parents should bring their children only on easy and low itineraries with little elevation.
2.   Good equipment is necessary, even for a short walk; good shoes adapted to the trails, warm and waterproof clothes.
3.   In the mountains, the weather changes rapidly. Within an hour, sun and heat may be replaced by snow and coldness.
4.   A ravine or gully covered with snow is very slippery, as well as a grassy slope; flower picking can turn into a disaster.
5.   All the tracks require intensive care (digging and repairing works); do not take the short cuts which soon develop into scars which canalize the rainwater thus deteriorating the trails.
6.   A picnic in the mountains or in a refuge is pleasant. Bring a plastic bag with you and take your rubbish back to the valley. The site will remain neat.
7.   Do not underestimate the length of an itinerary. You must plan to be back early, in order not to be overtaken by nightfall.
8.   In the mountains, there are hidden dangers, even on the well marked-out paths (forest works, repair works...). You must enquire and ask the qualified persons.
9.   When the goal of your hike is a refuge, you must remember that it is not easy and that good Alpine experience is necessary. You should be accompanied either by a guide or other qualified person.
10.   You must always advise your hotel or friends where you plan to go before leaving.

Average Walking Time

The times suggested for each walk are, inevitably, compromises. The ability and the desire to walk quickly and continuously, particularly up steep ascents and, indeed, to descend at speed over rough ground, vary enormously from individual to individual. These times are for the hypothetical 'average' walker, stopping occasionally for breath, to admire the view, and to take occasional photographs. Meal stops and other significant breaks are not included.

The Area of Haute-Savoie

General

The département of Haute-Savoie is big and beautiful. From Lac Léman in the north almost to Aix-les-Bains in the south, from Bellegarde in the west to the crowning glories of Mont Blanc in the south-east corner, there is very little which is in any way dull or unattractive, with the possible exception of the valley of the river Arve between Cluses and Annemasse. Whilst the finest scenery is without doubt the various mountain *massifs*, there is much else to admire, including the comparatively gentle countryside to the west around Rumilly, a good market town, and also the south of Lac Léman, known as Chablais. Several of the rivers have impressive gorges, in some cases privately owned and made accessible, at a price, by constructed walkways.

Much of the département is covered by forest, reaching high up the mountain slopes and clinging precariously to craggy cliffs. Most areas have a good mixture of trees and the autumn colours are spectacular. Plant life is also rich, the Alpine pastures living up to their reputation over a long flowering season. Even in mid October there are still plants in flower at surprisingly high altitudes.

The beautiful Annecy lake is the only large sheet of water wholly within Haute-Savoie, but several miles of the southern shore of the vast Lac Léman (known as Lac Genève to the Swiss) constitute the northern boundary, and there are smaller lakes in attractive surroundings which often provide a good focal point for walks.

The natural beauty of the département is undoubtedly enhanced by its buildings. Small châteaux, villages with *bulbe* bell towers and old houses, Alps with chalets looking just like illustrations from children's books, all play their part. It should be said that, as is the case in every country, not *all* the man-made structures contribute: the fringes of some of the towns are, to say the least, nondescript. Industrial estates on approach roads are clearly a necessity, but little effort seems to be made to provide screening. Perhaps worst of all is the approach from the west to Chamonix, most glorious of mountain areas. Whether by road or rail there is no avoiding the monstrous and noxious industrial complex at Chedde, blocking as it does the only valley giving access. But, as has been said, Haute-Savoie is big, and the beauty far outweighs these niggling irritations.

History

Curiously, Savoy has been a permanent part of France only since 1860, following a ballot of the inhabitants which gave an overwhelming majority for the union. Prior to that date, its strategic position, controlling the passes across the Alps, had ensured a fairly turbulent history, periods of independence alternating with periods of occupation by the French. From the early eighteenth century, Savoy and Sardinia together formed the kingdom of Sardinia which belonged to the Holy Roman Empire until independence was achieved in 1815.

Climate

As Haute-Savoie is much further south than the UK, higher summer temperatures are experienced. These are mitigated over much of the département by altitude, nevertheless, many will find that June to August are too hot for hard walking to be really enjoyable.

Conversely, winter imposes altogether different conditions and very few of the walks in this book would be advisable or even possible for ordinary walkers once the snow has arrived in early winter. Spring and autumn are delightful, but do remember that in the higher places snow will still be melting well into the month of June. In summer, Haute-Savoie enjoys a broadly Continental climate with less of the tempering effect of the sea than is found in the UK; it is hot in summer and cold in winter, but with the generally low rainfall of such a climate increased by the presence of mountains. It can be quite wet from time to time and thunderstorms are common. This type of climate also has a greater temperature contrast between day and night, and at some times of the year warm, sunny days are followed by cold, frosty nights.

It is not difficult to obtain local weather forecasts, which are particularly useful in mountain areas. Every tourist office and many hotels and *gîtes* have this information and a simple telephone call to Chamonix 50 53 03 40 is a good alternative.

Clothing, Equipment and Maps

Clothing

The choice of clothing for country and mountain walking is a matter of common sense. It should keep the wearer adequately warm, be sufficiently loose to permit movement and overall comfort, and keep out the wind and weather over the wide range of conditions found in a mountain area such as Haute-Savoie. Assuming that mountain walking in winter is not contemplated, the requirements are much the same as for the UK; a lightweight wind and waterproof cagoule with a hood over a sweater will generally suffice. A spare sweater should be carried for the lower temperatures at high level.

Not all walkers like the extra impediment to progress imposed by waterproof overtrousers, but others do prefer not to suffer occasionally soggy undertrousers! Excellent purpose-made trousers are available from specialist shops and suppliers, but garments in strong washable cotton, or corduroy for colder conditions, are perfectly adequate. In any case, trousers should be roomy rather than tight fitting. Having said all this, for a great deal of the time the sun will shine and the walker will perspire to the extent that minimal clothing is required. In these circumstances no doubt many will prefer to walk in shorts, hoping that the knees will not be needed for scrambling on rocks and that a lost path will not result in crossing beds of nettles!

In recent years, fabrics such as Gore-tex have been developed and are now used for the more expensive cagoules, combining excellent waterproofing with 'breathability', allowing the passage of perspiration. Even more expensive are parkas, of similar material but incorporating down or other high quality insulation. For the walking described in this book, more basic cagoules are perfectly adequate and, quite apart from the price, the extra weight of an insulated parka can hardly be justified.

By definition, the most important part of a walker's clothing must be his or her footwear. As in the case of cagoules, high technology has arrived, and the basic leather boot with its 'commando' sole must now compete with a whole range of more sophisticated products. Those who walk comparatively infrequently and not in severe conditions will be perfectly well served by low-price boots, but for more demanding walking, it is worth paying rather more for such refinements as double-density soles and permeable linings, which add considerably to comfort. Having walked for many years in the UK, particularly in the Lake District, I am not an advocate of the so-called 'summer boot', which pays little regard to waterproofing; even in Haute-Savoie I did manage to find wet snow and the odd swamp. It goes without saying that boots should be as light in weight as is consistent with the possession of firm soles and strong but flexible leather uppers, giving good support to the ankles.

Having strongly recommended boots for walking in Haute-Savoie, I recognise that some walkers will prefer stout shoes and will manage most of these walks quite well so shod. There is also a current trend to use soft-soled footwear such as trainers, but to feel the outline of every stone and pebble must surely be a disadvantage over the course of a walk of any substance. Whatever footwear you eventually choose, it is essential to allow room for good socks. If two pairs are worn at least one pair must be of the thick 'Harris' or similar material. In heavy rain or snow, gaiters may be worn to protect the tops of the boots.

Equipment

Equipment has to be carried and there is every incentive to keep it to a minimum. In addition to one or more extra sweaters, the following list includes the items which most walkers will wish to carry with them on day walks:

Food and drink, with a little extra for possible emergencies (The extra food will probably include high-energy items such as chocolate.)
Maps
Compass
Pathmaster guide
Whistle
Torch
Survival bag – obviously this is not really necessary for most of these walks, but it is not a bad thing to leave it in the rucksack. It is not very heavy and it will always be there just in case.
Basic first aid – antiseptic, bandage, sticking plasters, elasticated bandage, insect sting relief
Insect repellant
Lip salve
Sun cream
Sunglasses

Kendal mint cake or glucose tablets for instant energy
Hat, if hot sunshine is anticipated
Gloves are unlikely to be needed between spring and autumn
In addition to the above, camera and binoculars will add to the enjoyment of many walkers

Equipment is normally carried in a rucksack, and these come in all shapes and sizes. A rucksack with a frame is always more comfortable to carry but will weigh a little more than an equivalent sack without one. The type with an external frame is particularly good, as the weight is placed high on the wearer's back. The frameless type needs careful packing, so that soft articles lie against the back. For one or two persons, essential equipment can be comfortably accommodated in a small rucksack, assuming the walks are being done on a 'day-walking' basis. If the walker is moving on, for example along a long-distance footpath, staying at different hostels or *gîtes* each night, then a much bigger rucksack capable of holding spare clothing and other gear is required.

'Backpacking' on a completely independent basis, carrying a tent and all camping necessities, imposes even greater carrying requirements. Such walkers will have worked out their requirements from experience and will need no further advice.

Maps

To reach Haute-Savoie by road and for overall planning, small-scale maps such as the ubiquitous Michelin 1:200,000 series will be adequate. For many parts of France there are large composite sheets which each cover the area of several standard sheets and are better value for money. Sheet No. 244 *Rhône-Alpes* contains Haute-Savoie (except for the part adjacent to Lac Léman), and a good deal more besides. The missing part is included in composite Sheet No. 243 *Bourgogne–Franche-Comté* and in individual Sheet No. 70 *Beaune–Evian*.

For the actual walking, there is a choice of *Institut Géographique National* (IGN), the French equivalent of the Ordnance Survey maps, at scales of 1:50,000 and 1:25,000. Whilst the latter is clearly the better scale for detail, there is a particular series of maps at 1:50,000 in the *Editions Didier Richard*, giving prominence to *randonnées pédestres* (signposted footpaths) and ski-runs. Sheet Nos. 2, 3 and 8 cover Haute-Savoie, with some overlapping, and all the walks in this book. This special series does have some maps at the better scale of 1:25,000, but covering only part of the area. Stanfords, 14 Long

Acre, London W1, are stockists of IGN and other French maps.

After the light colouring and general clarity of the British Ordnance Survey, it does take time to become accustomed to the comparatively muddy appearance of the IGN maps. In the special edition, footpaths are shown by a very clear blue line, but roads are left uncoloured and are not easy to follow. The 20 metres interval contours are packed very closely indeed in much of Haute-Savoie. Perseverance is required, as these maps do contain a great deal of useful information and, with some practice, do eventually become comprehensible.

Before Departure and Health-care

Some aspects of preparing for an overseas holiday are drudgery; motoring insurance, cross channel or air bookings, and money come immediately to mind.

On the other hand, there is distinct pleasure in obtaining maps, guides, and more general books on the chosen area.. Having scoured the local library and bookshops, do not hesitate to write to the tourist office in any town which you propose to visit. The inclusion of an International Reply Coupon, obtainable at post offices, will almost certainly bring a speedy and helpful reply. A precise address is not essential; *Office de Tourisme* or *Syndicat d'Initiative*, with the name of the town and the department will find its destination.

Motorists will need to take the vehicle registration documents and driving licence and must inform their insurance company, which may or may not issue a standard 'green card' and may or may not make a charge. Extra equipment will include at least a red triangle and a spare set of light bulbs. Those towing caravans should, in addition, fix extra rear-view mirror and consider taking out an extra insurance package such as the 'Red Pennant' of the Caravan Club or the RAC or AA alternative. These packages include comprehensive benefits; they are not cheap but are certainly very good for the peace of mind whilst touring abroad.

Money has never been easier to arrange. The former restriction to travellers' cheques and cash has gone and most major credit cards are widely accepted in France. The services provided by banks are duplicated by 'change' offices in larger towns and cities, whilst the Eurocheque scheme enables a bank to cash an ordinary UK cheque on production of a banker's card, in addition to the normal facility of cashing travellers' cheques in sterling or francs and possibly sterling in cash. The banks are generally open from Monday to Friday, 9am to 4pm, but, like so many shops, do close for a long lunch break. Do not forget to take your passport!

Form E111, obtained free from the DoH offices, is the essential requirement if use is made of state medical services in France. The French version of the NHS has general practitioner and hospital arrangements similar to those in the UK, but payment is likely to be requested on delivery of a service. Use of the E111 allows a claim for reimbursement to be made. As an alternative, private insurance arrangements may be made before departure. It is usual for cases needing speedy attention to go direct to hospital emergency (*urgences*) departments.

Every town and large village has at least one *pharmacie*, very prominent with its green cross, usually illuminated and occasionally flashing. A pharmacist will always give first aid and will also advise on remedies for minor ailments and on such matters as which of the great variety of wild fungi are edible and which are poisonous. There are two types of poisonous snake in France. Pharmacists stock the serum necessary for speedy treatment of anyone unfortunate enough to be bitten and it is also available as a kit for self-injection.

Travelling to Haute-Savoie

Air

The only international airport serving Haute-Savoie is actually in Switzerland – 6km (4 miles) to the west of Geneva (tel: 41 22 98 11 22) with direct flights from several UK airports. All Haute-Savoie is within 65km (40 miles) or so of Geneva.

Rail

France is famous for its very fast *trains de grande vitesse* (TGV), now reaching a large number of major towns and cities. The hub of the system is, inevitably, Paris, easily reached by rail from the channel ports. Through TGV services operate to Annecy (in less than 4 hours), Geneva (for Thonon-les-Bains and Evian-les-Bains), Cluses (for Morzine, Samoëns and Taninges), and to Le Fayet/St Gervais-les-Bains (for Megève and Chamonix).

Quite apart from the TGVs, other rail services in Europe's largest network are generally good, and the following special services might well be of interest.

'Motorail' is available from Paris or Lille to Le Fayet/St Gervais-les-Bains and from Paris to Evian-les-Bains. Overnight accommodation on these trains comprises a variety of 1st and 2nd class sleepers and couchettes, and Continental breakfast is included in the price. An added inducement is discounted fare on Sealink and Hoverspeed cross-Channel services.

'Train plus Auto' is the result of a partnership between SNCF (French railways) and Avis. Before travelling it is possible, at more than 2,000 railway stations including those at the Channel ports, to book the use of a car at any one of about 200 stations throughout France. With some exceptions, cars taken at one of these stations may be left at any other of the 200 at the end of the hire period, if desired. In Haute-Savoie, the following stations are included in the scheme: Bellegarde, Annemasse, Thonon-les-Bains, Evian-les-Bains, Cluses, Sallanches, Le Fayet/St Gervais-les-Bains, Chamonix and Annecy. Cars may also be reserved by telephone on either 05 05 05 11 or 16(1)46 09 92 12.

'Railrover' type tickets are worth investigation by walkers who intend to travel by train. The best known of this type of ticket is the European 'Interail', beloved of students and other young persons, but there are others which could be of more direct relevance to a trip to Haute-Savoie. The 'France–Vacances' pass offers unlimited travel on any four days during a period of fifteen days for £64 (child £32) 2nd class, or £90 (child £45) 1st class. Alternatively for nine days travel during a period of one month, the cost is £108 (child £54) 2nd class, or £160 (child £80) 1st class. (The above prices were correct in 1989.) There are no less than nine bonuses attached to the purchase of a France–Vacances pass, including a reduction in the cross-Channel Hoverspeed fare, a reduction in car-hire rates, a discount on some hotel prices, and travel concessions within Paris. The cheaper pass would appeal to visitors travelling to Haute-Savoie by train, returning within fifteen days, and enjoying two full days of rail excursions during the holiday. At £64 it must be a bargain.

Express coaches run from London to Haute-Savoie every day from the beginning of April to the end of September. This service is provided by the National Express/Eurolines organisation which reaches over sixty destinations throughout France. Service No. 131 travels via Dover, Paris and Lyon to Grenoble, Chambéry, Annecy, Annemasse (for Thonon-les-Bains and Evian-les-Bains) and Chamonix. Although the route via Grenoble is not very direct, the overall journey time of 19 hours 50 minutes to Annecy and 22 hours 20 minutes to Chamonix is creditable. Adult fares (1989) are £79 return to Annecy and £87 return to Chamonix, with children at half-price and small concessions for youths or students.

Having considered these methods of reaching Haute-Savoie, the likelihood is that, for reasons of flexibility of travel times, for independent travel within the département, and for a luggage-carrying capacity, most British visitors will travel by car. For those in a hurry and willing to pay tolls, which do mount up over a long journey (Calais to Annecy is about 800km (500 miles)), particularly if a caravan is towed, the *autoroutes* (motorways) are recommended. Most of the network has less traffic than is found on motorways in the UK and every 20km (12 miles) or so there is an *aire de repos* – a pull-off picnic area with toilets, usually well laid out with shrubs and other landscaping. Approximately every third *aire de repos* is a more comprehensive service area with fuel and catering. For Haute-Savoie, from just outside Calais take the A26 heading towards Reims. Transfer to the A4 near Reims, leaving the *autoroute* near Châlons sur Marne, and following the *route nationale* RN44, then the RN74 through Vitry-le-François, St Dizier, Chaumont and Langres, until reaching an *autoroute* access to the north of Dijon. This is the A31, heading towards Beaune, and joining the A6. If keeping to the *autoroute* as much as possible, carry on to Mâcon and then take the A40 towards Geneva. A more direct route is to leave the *autoroute* at Tournus and to follow the D975 towards Bourg-en-Bresse, joining the A40 for Geneva north of that town, which is thereby by-passed. The A40 does have a gap near Bellegarde, the missing link being under construction in 1989.

Annecy may be reached by rejoining the A40 and changing to the A41 near La Roche-sur-Foron. However, it is probably preferable to take the RN 508 from Bellegarde, direct to Annecy, via Frangy. For Chamonix, rejoin the A40 after the gap and carry on to the end of the *autoroute* near St Gervais-les-Bains. RN205 continues as a good, dual-carriageway route, direct to Chamonix. For Morzine, Samoëns and Taninges leave the A40 at Cluses and follow the D902. For Samoëns, a right turn on to the D907 in Taninges is required.

Motorists not wishing to use *autoroutes* have a much greater variety of route and scenery available. One of the joys of travelling in France is to discover minor roads, largely free of traffic, and often running surprisingly straight for a considerable distance. (Having said that, I have never found any joy in major or minor roads between Calais and St Quentin and consider the toll for using this part of the A26 to be money well spent.) If the Channel is crossed to Boulogne or Dunkirk, there are good links into the route described above, via the A25 and the A1 in the latter case, and by the RN42 from Boulogne. From Dieppe or Caen, the A13 can be used as far as Paris, where it connects with the A6 to Beaune.

Addresses and telephone numbers

French Railways Ltd, 179 Piccadilly, London W1V 0BA, tel: 071 409 3518.

Railway information within Haute-Savoie, tel: 50 66 50 50.

Railway reservations: Annecy, tel: 50 51 66 66; Chamonix, tel: 50 53 00 44; Le Fayet/St Gervais les Bains, tel: 50 78 23 46; Cluses, tel: 50 98 00 83; Thonon-les-Bains, tel: 50 71 31 98; Evian-les-Bains, tel: 50 75 25 26.

National Express/Eurolines: 52 Grosvenor Gardens, Victoria, London SW1; Coach Travel Centre, 13 Regent Street, London SW1; Victoria Coach Station, Buckingham Palace Road, London SW1.

Bookings may be made in person at any of the above addresses or through local National Express agents. Additionally, there are enquiry centres:-

London	tel: 071 730 0202
Birmingham	tel: 021 622 4373
Bournemouth	tel: 0202 21481
Bristol	tel: 0272 541022
Cambridge	tel: 0223 460711
Exeter	tel: 0392 215454
Leeds	tel: 0532 460011
Liverpool	tel: 051 709 6481
Manchester	tel: 061 228 3881
Newcastle	tel: 091 261 6077
Nottingham	tel: 0602 585317
Oxford	tel: 0865 791579
Peterborough	tel: 0733 237141
Sheffield	tel: 0742 754905

Where to Stay

Haute-Savoie is a prime tourist area and there is no shortage of accommodation for visitors. However, as many of the resorts among the mountains are geared primarily to the winter sports season, some hotels do close for the rest of the year, whilst even more hotels close for a 'low' season from September or October to December.

Hotels

All grades of hotel are available, from the small *pension* to the very grand indeed, such as *L'Abbaye* at Talloires. In France, it is usual for hotels to display their range of prices outside and the price, inclusive of tax and service, for a particular room inside the door of that room. It is expected that prospective guests will wish to inspect a room and may well ask to see alternative rooms before deciding whether or not to stay. Breakfast, always of the Continental variety, is charged separately. The combined price for bed and breakfast is almost always less than would be charged in a British hotel of equivalent standard. For example, a 2-star hotel in an average situation is likely to cost from £10 to £15 per person for a couple sharing a double or twin-bedded room with private bath or shower.

The organisation of *Logis et Auberges de France*, which reached its 40th anniversary in 1989, is justifiably popular with British visitors. The *logis* are 1- or 2-star hotels of modest size, offering predictable and guaranteed standards of comfort, whilst the *auberges* are more simple with correspondingly lower prices. Almost all *logis* and *auberges* are family owned and managed and, in contrast to the frequently anonymous and monotonous sameness of many large company hotels, there is great diversity of buildings and style. Very few towns of any significance are now without at least one hotel affiliated to the organisation, the national total having exceeded 4,600. There are *logis* and *auberges* throughout Haute-Savoie; Annecy has five, Chamonix has two, with others in nearby villages, whilst Morzine has no less than thirteen.

There are many groups based in the UK who now either own or have booking arrangements with hotels in France. Their contacts range from luxury hotels such as Holiday Inns and Novotels to organisations which will arrange long or short stays in quite modest hotels, very often on a sequential basis to facilitate touring.

For those who dislike making independent arrangements, hotel accommodation can be combined with travel by air, rail or coach in packages available from several UK-based companies. Centres in Haute-Savoie include Annecy, Chamonix and Evian-les-Bains, and names, addresses and telephone numbers of the companies concerned are listed in the *Guide for the Traveller in France* , issued free by the French Government Tourist Office in London.

Guest Rooms

In order to supplement the available accommodation, particularly in smaller villages, there is a scheme known as *'Café-Couette'* (literally 'coffee and quilt'). Over 1,500 rooms in private houses throughout France are available for guests for long or short stays. The organisation claims that all the houses included are of high quality, offering a very different style of holiday experience and, in particular, bringing the visitor into closer contact with friendly, hospitable French people. There are three grades and prices, all guaranteed to meet the standards set by the organisation. The basic grade offers a warm welcome, comfort and an attractive location for £12.50 per person for a couple sharing a double room. The middle grade adds a private bath and toilet and possibly a swimming pool or tennis court. The top grade further adds either a particularly luxurious or historic building. Continental breakfast is included in all classes. There is a price supplement of about sixty per cent for single accommodation. A membership card is required; this can be purchased and advance bookings can be made through Bed and Breakfast (France) PO Box 66, 94 Bell Street, Henley-on-Thames, Oxon RG9 1XS, tel: 0491 578803. At present, Haute-Savoie is not well provided with *café-couette* rooms but the scheme is still expanding.

There are many rooms let on a more casual basis, particularly in small towns and villages that are not well provided with hotels. It is usual to ask at a café, where one or more rooms might well be used for letting; if not, the proprietor will probably know of someone who does have a vacant room. Prices will be low, but furnishings may be sparse and not in first-class condition, and visitors should not hesitate to refuse an unacceptable room.

Villas and Chalets

Haute-Savoie has self-catering accommodation in profusion, particularly in the winter sport areas. Each local tourist office has lists available, normally with a fair amount of detail including: number of rooms, maximum sleeping capacity, name and telephone number of owner, prices for different times of the year, and sometimes a grading system – '*simple, confortable, très confortable*'. Occasionally, photographs of the various properties are included.

The *Gîtes de France* is a well-established organisation, with an illustrated handbook listing over 2,000 properties to let, usually on a weekly basis, and with its own section at the French Government Tourist Office in London. Prices average £90 – £200 for a house for 4–6 persons and all bookings can be made in Britain.

Gîtes d'Étape

These establishments are totally different from the *gîtes* mentioned above.

They are not unlike youth hostels, providing simple accommodation very suitable for walkers. Many are converted farm buildings, whilst others comprise part of an hotel or large house. The sleeping accommodation is usually in dormitories, visitors using their own sleeping bags; kitchen, wash-rooms, and showers are provided on a communal basis. There may or may not be a resident warden and if there is, meals may be offered. A maximum stay of three nights is specified and the cost is between £2 and £3 per person per night. The organisation is expanding and attempts are being made to establish *gîtes* at reasonable intervals along all *grande randonnée* routes. *Gîtes* are fairly plentiful in Haute-Savoie, particularly in the Chamonix valley.

Youth Hostels

Youth hostels are concentrated more in the larger towns than is the case in the UK. A list can be obtained from the Youth Hostels Association or direct from the Fédération Unie des Auberges de la Jeunesse, 6 rue Mesnil, 75116 Paris. There are youth hostels at Annecy, Morzine and near to Chamonix (Les Pélérins).

Refuges (shelters)

Basic accommodation is provided at a large number of refuges among the mountains, most operated by the Club Alpin Français, the sites being shown on IGN maps. The conditions of use vary greatly, some always being open, whilst others have a definite 'season'. There may or may not be a resident warden and some refuges may even be free of charge. Those situated in popular places, such as the route of the Tour de Mont Blanc, will normally be full and a place should be reserved in advance. Telephone numbers are available at local tourist offices. Walkers intending to use refuges are advised to obtain detailed information from CAF which has an office at 136 Avenue Michel-Croz, 74400, Chamonix, tel: 50 53 16 03.

Camping Sites

In France, almost all organised sites accept caravans, motor caravans, and tents. There are more than 11,000 such sites, all graded in accordance with the quantity and quality of sanitary and other amenities. The 'star' rating and the charges should always be displayed by site entrance or office. A comprehensive list is published by the French Federation of Camping and Caravanning, Springdene, Shepherds Way, Fairlight, Sussex TN35 4BB at

£6.95, but most visitors will probably prefer to use a more selective guide such as those issued by the Caravan Club, the AA or Michelin. The French Government Tourist Office has a departmental list for Haute-Savoie and local lists are available at tourist offices.

Prices are regulated in accordance with the classification and the total cost is usually the sum of the pitch, plus car, plus persons. Sometimes pitch and car are combined. Mains electrical hook-up is extra and is comparatively expensive, particularly as the amperage is always restricted and many sites offer only 2 to 6 amps.

The typical cost for a caravan or tent, with car and 2 persons, would be £4 – £5 per night on a 3-star site and £2.50 – £3.50 on a 2-star site. Each child would add 30p to 70p to this total and an electrical hook-up would cost a further £1 – £2, depending on amperage. In 'low' season (May, June, September, October) charges may be slightly reduced. Most sites in France are well managed but in popular tourist areas they can become crowded in July and August. Even when a site displays the '*complet*' (full) sign, backpackers with a small tent may well find that the management is willing to fit them in somewhere. Outside the months of July and August sites are generally quiet, many not opening until May or June, and closing again in September or early October, despite the frequently beautiful spring and autumnal weather.

Annecy and the settlements around the lake are well provided with sites, those close to the lake shore being the most likely to be full or crowded. Chamonix and its valley also have excellent sites, 'Les Deux Glaciers' at Les Bossons having a longer opening season that most. The municipal site at Taninges is also recommended for a long opening season and very good value for money. Several well-equipped sites open in both summer and again in winter (*caravaneige*) for the winter sports season, with periods of closure in between. Possession of an international camping *carnet* is advised; it does result in a discount of about ten per cent at some sites and avoids having to leave your passport at the site office. *Carnets* are obtainable through caravan and camping organisations in the UK.

In many rural areas, the official camping sites are supplemented by *camping à la ferme* (on the farm), small-scale sites with simple facilities, which are ideal for backpackers. As the most attractive parts of Haute-Savoie are mountainous and the farming is consequently specialised Alpine, there are very few of these sites.

Camping *sauvage* (wild – not on a site) is not really encouraged, particularly in forests, and is forbidden in designated National and Regional Parks. Nevertheless, in remote areas, such as high in the mountains, a small tent in a discreet position will have tacit acceptance.

Local Transport

Rail

Like most mountain areas, Haute-Savoie is not particularly well served by railways. A main line crosses the middle of the département, from Bellegarde to Le Fayet/St Gervais-les-Bains, also connecting with Geneva on the Swiss side of the frontier. A second important line runs north to south from Grenoble and Chambéry via Aix-les-Bains to Annecy, then connecting with the other main line at La Roche-sur-Foron. From a junction at Annemasse, a branch line serves Thonon-les-Bains and Evian-les-Bains, whilst from Le Fayet/St Gervais-les-Bains a metre gauge line runs the length of the Chamonix valley before climbing steeply over the frontier and descending to Martigny in Switzerland. For walkers, the Chamonix line is likely to be the most useful. There are several small stations and unstaffed halts along the way and their use is suggested in several of the walks. The service is reasonably frequent and timetables are widely available at stations and local tourist offices. The other line with a local service is the branch in the north of the département, close to Lac Léman. The trains are less frequent, there are few intermediate stations and, like the lines running north and south from Annecy, this line is likely to be more useful for longer distance excursions than as an adjunct to walking. In respect of the Chamonix line, a *Passeport pour les Cimes* (peaks) is available, allowing seven days unrestricted travel between Sallanches and Vallorcine for 100 francs per person or 200 francs for a family. A similar passport can be purchased for the Swiss section of this line. (Telephone numbers for information and reservations are given on page 21.)

Buses

Local bus services are many and varied; timetables are essential and are obtainable from the offices of the bus companies and from local tourist offices. The services available are:

Annecy – urban services	SIBRA
Annecy – Veyrier – Talloires – Angon	CROLARD
Annecy – Sévrier – St Jorioz	CROLARD
Annecy – Duingt – Lathuile – Faverges – Albertville	CROLARD
Annecy – Thônes	CROLARD
Annecy – La Roche-sur-Foron – Geneva	FROSSARD
Annecy – Aix-les-Bains – Chambéry	FROSSARD

Annecy – Thonon-les-Bains – Evian – St Gingolph	FROSSARD
Sallanches – Le Fayet – Plâteau d'Assy – Lac Vert	SAT
Sallanches – St Gervais – Les Contamines – N D de la Gorge	SAT
Le Fayet – Sallanches – Combloux	SAT
Le Fayet – St Gervais – Megève – Praz sur Arly	SAT
Plan d'Eau – Sallanches – Megève – Praz sur Arly	SAT
Praz sur Arly – Megève – Chamonix – Aosta (Italy)	SAT
Praz sur Arly – Megève – St Gervais – Chamonix	SAT
Chamonix – Sallanches – Cluses – Annecy	SAT
Chamonix – St Gervais – Megève – Albertville – Grenoble	SAT
Chamonix – St Gervais – Ugine – Annecy	SAT
Chamonix – Le Fayet – St Gervais – Les Contamines	SAT
Chamonix – Sallanches – Cluses – Geneva	SAT/GENEVE EXCURSIONS
Chamonix – Le Fayet – Plateau d'Assy – Lac Vert	SAT
Les Contamines – St Gervais – Sallanches – Cluses – Geneva	SAT
Megève – Mont d'Arbois – Côte 2000	SAT
Megève – Rochebrune – Faucigny	SAT
Chamonix – valley service from col des Montets to Les Houches	CHAMONIX BUS
Cluses – Taninges – Samoëns – Sixt	SAT
Cluses – Les Gets – Morzine – Avoriaz	SAT
Geneva – Taninges – Samoëns – Sixt – Fer à Cheval	SAT
Bonneville – Cluses – Megève	BORINI/TOURISCAR
Bonneville – Cluses – Chamonix	CROLARD/SAT
Taninges – Praz de Lys (winter only)	SAT
Geneva – Taninges – Morzine – Avoriaz (winter only)	SAT
Thonon-les-Bains – Morzine – Les Gets	SAT
Thonon-les-Bains – Morzine – Avoriaz	SAT
Geneva – Thonon-les-Bains – Evian – St Gingolph	FROSSARD
Thonon-les-Bains – Evian	FROSSARD
Thonon-les-Bains – Evian – St Gingolph	FROSSARD
Thonon-les-Bains – Evian – Thollon – La Joux	FROSSARD

It must be emphasised that many of these services run to timetables which are very seasonal and that at some times of the year the service is extremely limited.

Addresses and telephone numbers:

SIBRA – Bonlieu open-air car park Annecy 50 51 70 33.
VOYAGES CROLARD – Gare Routière Sud Annecy 50 45 08 12;
Thônes – 50 02 00 11;
La Clusaz – 50 02 40 11.
FROSSARD VOYAGES – Gare Routière Sud Annecy 50 45 73 90;
7 Place des Arts, Thonon-les-Bains 50 26 41 32;
Quai Blonay, Evian-les-Bains 50 75 01 62.
SAT VOYAGES – 3 Impasse du Mt Blanc, Cluses 50 98 01 67.
CHAMONIX BUS – Place de l'Église, Chamonix 50 53 05 55.

Food and Drink

Almost every visitor to France puts food and wine (not necessarily in that order) high on his list of attractions. The quality and diversity of both over the length and breadth of this great country are truly remarkable. Most visitors will need little advice on the generality of either gastronomy or wine; suffice it to say that the widest selection of wines and spirits, and the keenest prices, are always to be found in hypermarkets. Beer is also extremely cheap, whether bought in litres or in the popular twelve or twenty-four packs of quarter-litre bottles. On such indispensable items as cheese and *pâtisserie*, the hypermarket again will score heavily on choice and price. For fruit and vegetables the local markets come into their own; nearly all towns have a market day which is worth noting both for practical shopping reasons and as part of the holiday entertainment.

In Haute-Savoie, Annecy has Rallye and Auchan hypermarkets, and there are the large supermarkets Provencia and Super U at Sévrier and St Jorioz respectively. Surprisingly for such a popular tourist area, the Chamonix valley has no hypermarket, the best supermarkets being Codec just outside Chamonix and Banco at Les Houches. Morzine and Samoëns have Banco supermarkets, whilst Taninges has Codec. Châtel near Abondance has a Banco and Thonon-les-Bains has a real hypermarket – Euromarché – on its eastern fringe. With regard to local specialities, Haute-Savoie has a reputation for cheese – especially fondue and raclette – and there is good freshwater fish, the small perch fillets being particularly recommended. The most notable cheeses are Tomme and Reblochon, and both are sold direct from many farms. Each type has several varieties, and one of the best Tommes is Tomme d'Abondance, specifically from the valley of the same name, which is also distinguished by having its own breed of cows. Equally esteemed are varieties of Gruyère cheese, particularly Beaufort, said to be known at the time of the Romans, and Emmental. Goat cheese (*fromage de chèvre*) is also produced locally.

Savoy is not one of the best-known wine producing areas in France and exports to the UK are fairly minimal. However, several good white wines are produced and are widely available locally. Although having no pretension to greatness, these wines have something of the character of Alsace wires and are certainly superior to the lower-priced, rather anonymous wines, which form the bulk of everyday drinking. Typical labels include Aligoté, Abymes, Apremont, Chignin, Jacquère and the sparkling Crépy. There are also good red wines including Gamay, Pinot and Mondeuse.

Finding acceptable restaurants should present no problem, except perhaps out of season, most hotels having menus at 60 francs (£6) upwards for three or four courses. Choosing *à la carte* is always more expensive, but more ambitious dishes will be offered. For more casual eating, rather akin to our pub meals, a *plat du jour* is offered at many establishments which are primarily bars; this 'plat' will cost from 30 francs (£3) to 40 francs (£4).

The mark-up on drinks in hotels and restaurants is always considerable, and the best buy is often the house wine, sometimes served in a *pichet* (jug). Beer prices are particularly disparate. A quarter-litre bottle costing 15p in the hypermarket will be not less than 80p, and occasionally £1.20 in a bar or hotel.

Fast food catering has, fortunately, not overwhelmed towns in France to the extent that it has in the UK and other European countries. It is still comparatively rare to see the garish neon signs nor is there the equivalent of British fish and chip shops or Chinese take-aways, other than from stalls along the main roads. The best examples of the French version of mass-produced catering are, in fact, the restaurants or cafeterias attached to some hypermarkets. The restaurant at Euromarché at Thonon-les-Bains is a good example, doing its basic job with efficiency and not a little style.

General Information

Tourist Offices

Of the great number of tourist offices in Haute-Savoie, the following are most relevant to the walks in this book:

Annecy   tel: 50 45 00 33

Thônes	tel: 50 02 00 26
La Clusaz	tel: 50 02 60 92
St Jorioz	tel: 50 68 17 07
Talloires	tel: 50 60 70 64
Chamonix	tel: 50 53 20 00
Argentière	tel: 50 54 02 14
Les Houches	tel: 50 55 50 62
Morzine	tel: 50 79 03 45
Samoëns	tel: 50 34 40 28
Taninges	tel: 50 34 25 05
Evian-les-Bains	tel: 50 75 04 26
Thonon-les-Bains	tel: 50 71 50 88
Abondance	tel: 50 73 02 90

Railway Stations

The following stations may be of use: Annecy, Chamonix, Argentière, La Joux, Les Tines, Les Praz, Les Pélérins, Les Moussoux, Les Bossons, Taconnaz, Les Houches, Le Fayet, Sallanches, Cluses, Thonon-les-Bains, Evian-les-Bains.

Emergency Services

Police	tel: 17] Free calls
Fire Brigade	tel: 18]
Mountain Rescue	tel: 50 53 16 89
Chamonix Hospital	tel: 50 53 04 74

Other Useful Information

British Consul, 24 rue Childebert, 69288 Lyon, tel: 78 37 59 67.

Weather reports	tel: 50 53 03 40
Road Information	tel: 50 66 10 74
Company of mountain guides:	
Chamonix	tel: 50 53 00 88
Argentière	tel: 50 54 00 12
Les Houches	tel: 50 54 50 76
Taxis (Chamonix)	tel: 50 53 13 94
Alpine Museum, Chamonix	tel: 50 53 25 93
Chalet/laboratory Col des Montets	tel: 50 54 02 24

Mountain Museum, Les Houches	tel: 50 55 50 62
Youth hostel – Les Pélérins	tel: 50 53 14 52
Gendarmerie: Annecy	tel: 50 23 56 60
Chamonix	tel: 50 53 00 55
local police station, Annecy	tel: 50 51 32 54
local police station, Chamonix	tel: 50 53 10 97

Club Alpin Français (CAF) 136 Avenue Michel-Croz 74400; Chamonix Mt Blanc tel: 50 53 16 03.

Cableways/Chairlifts

Chamonix area:

Aiguille du Midi	tel: 50 53 30 80
Brévent	tel: 50 53 13 18
Flégère (Les Praz)	tel: 50 53 18 58
Glacier des Bossons(Les Bossons)	tel: 50 53 12 39
Montenvers	tel: 50 53 12 54
Planards (summer toboggans)	tel: 50 53 08 97
Col de Balme (Le Tour)	tel: 50 54 00 58
Grands Montets (Argentière)	tel: 50 54 00 71
Bellevue (Les Houches)	tel: 50 54 40 32
Prarion (Les Houches)	tel: 50 54 42 65

Mountain Railways

Chamonix – Montenvers	tel: 50 53 12 54
Le Fayet/St Gervais – Eagle's Nest(Tramway du Mt Blanc) tel: 50 78 27 23	

Using the Telephone

Public telephones in France are now generally efficient and the boxes do not seem to suffer greatly from vandalism, possibly because coin-box public phones are rapidly becoming extinct. Boxes are found more or less where you would expect – town centres, railway and bus stations, entrances to camping sites. With the demise of coin boxes, the purchase of a phone-card is strongly advised. This useful piece of plastic comes in two denominations, 40 francs (£4) and 90 francs (£9), and is simple to use, following the instructions in each phone box. Cards are obtained at newsagents' shops, *bar/tabacs*, tourist and post offices. Each call is debited on the card and the value remaining is clearly shown. Calls to the UK will soon diminish the value of a card, but a cheaper rate applies after 8pm. The appropriate international dialling code from France to the UK is 19 44, and the zero which is prefixed to the local dialling code is omitted (for example, all London numbers will start with 1 after dialling 19 44). From the UK to France, dial 010 33.

THE AREA

South-west Haute-Savoie

Annecy

As a centre for visitors to Haute-Savoie with a keen interest in walking, Annecy is an excellent choice. It is of medium, manageable size, with all the facilities which would be expected in a 'county' town – the *préfecture* is here – which is also a centre for the surrounding countryside and a major tourist resort.

Annecy's situation on the western fringe of the Alps allows quite easy access although it has to be said that the last few kilometres of the usual approach road from Bellegarde are less than pretty, due to badly screened industrial estates and excessive hoardings. Its setting, at the foot of a lake surrounded by mountains of a modest height, is beautiful, and the town itself is a fine mixture of old and new. With regard to the new, there are excellent shops with two out-of-town hypermarkets, railway and bus stations with good services, both local and distant, the Bonlieu centre with tourist office, library, theatre, fountains and extensive subterranean car parking, and good use of the lake frontage with a large marina. However, it is the old which really tips the scales in Annecy's favour. The old town is superb; not just the odd street with one or two self-consciously preserved old buildings, but a sizeable area nestling below the rock with the huge old château, and intersected by the flower-bedecked waterways carrying the outfall from the lake. It bustles with activity, particularly on the many market days, when the pavement cafés are at their most attractive. Much of the old town is pedestrianised and the visitor can admire the old buildings, soon becoming quite spoilt for choice. Churches abound; in the old town are the Cathedral St Pierre and the churches of St François, St Maurice, and Notre Dame-de-Liesse, with its neoclassical facade dating from the 1840s. On its hill behind the château, La Visitation commands attention, particularly at night, when its white spire is beautifully illuminated. The basilica was built in 1922 but was not finished and consecrated until 1949. The monastery of the Visitation is the headquarters of the monastic order founded in 1610 by St François de Sales and St Jeanne de Chantal, both of whom are buried there.

Other buildings of note include Le Palais de l'Isle, an oddly-shaped structure, very prominently situated between waterways. It has had several uses over nine centuries or so, and has been a prison, and a seat of the judiciary. It is now a museum with an exhibition displaying the history of Annecy and Savoy. The former town hall has a well-proportioned frontage and ornamental access stairways apparently much admired by Ruskin, whilst the former seat of the Bishops of Geneva has a long, more severe facade. The Hôtel de Sales has four small statues representing the four seasons; it was built by the Sales family in the seventeenth century and later became the headquarters of the Savoy Bank, which joined the Banque de France, after political union in 1860.

A short steep climb from the main thoroughfare of Rue St Clair reaches the château, a composite structure dating from many different periods. The large and impressive courtyard gives access to several museums, showing regional archaeology, ethnography and natural history, with particular reference to the way of life, the arts and traditions of Savoy. Each year there are various special exhibitions, both at the château and at the Conservatoire d'Art et d'Histoire de la Haute-Savoie, which is situated in a late seventeenth-century building at No. 18 Avenue de Trésun, near to the hospital and accessible by a direct link on foot from the château. A little further out of town, in the suburb of Seynod, is the 'Three Wars Museum', open daily throughout the year.

Whilst glorying in its past, Annecy is also anxious to show itself as a forward-looking town and resort. To this end, sporting facilities have not been neglected. The lake offers all the expected watersports such as sailing, windsurfing, skiing and fishing, with pedallos, small hire boats and regular excursions round the lake for the less sporting. There is golf, at a rather high price, at Talloires (tel: 50 60 12 89) and golf driving ranges at Gillon-Epagny and Giez. 'Mini-Golf' is provided at five of the lakeside villages, with bowling at Sévrier. Tennis is available at Annecy – Tennis Club des Marquisats (tel: 50 45 17 18) – and at virtually every village around the lake. There are two covered and one open-air swimming pool, whilst Annecy itself has three free supervised lakeside beaches and one where a charge is made. There are also beaches at various villages; the one at St Jorioz is probably the best. The lake water is claimed to be very pure; it certainly has a good clear appearance and in summer the water temperature is excellent for bathing.

Horse-riding enthusiasts are not neglected; Annecy has 'La Cravache d'Annecy' (tel: 50 45 32 38) and there are other centres at Talloires, Sévrier,

Chavanod, Argonay, Seynod and Doussard.

Lake fishing requires a carte from the Fédération de Pêche, 1 rue de l'Industrie à Annecy (tel: 50 45 26 90), also obtainable from shops selling fishing goods.

Bicycles may be hired at Annecy, Sévrier, St Jorioz, Annecy le Vieux and Talloires. There is a particularly good cycle route along the west side of the lake, most of the way being along a disused railway line, including a tunnel at Duingt.

As a resort Annecy is well provided with accommodation for visitors, ranging from good quality hotels to camping sites and a youth hostel, although it does become crowded in the summer season – the camping sites in particular have a short period of intense activity, followed by a few slack weeks in the autumn. Although there always seems to be a great deal of traffic, off-street car parking is provided on a fairly generous scale, and there are seven very central car parks, in respect of which a charge is made, totalling 1,842 spaces, and of these the Bonlieu car park is recommended. It is very central, not too difficult to find from the access roads from east or west sides of the lake, and usually seems to have available space as it is very much the biggest in town. The charges are comparable with those in a UK town of similar importance. More peripheral, there are eleven free car parks, with a total of 1,892 spaces.

With Annecy's wealth of attractions, it is hardly surprising that in high season there are daily organised excursions for visitors. For 20 francs a 2-hour guided tour of the old town is available and, for those walkers who appreciate the services of a guide, there are various mountain expeditions, some being easy, whilst others are ambitious trips to the *haute-montagne*. The majority are one-day walks, but there are some two-day excursions including a night in a refuge, offering a safe opportunity to sample life on the high mountain to those who would like to extend their range but would prefer to be with a guide. The programme is available at the Annecy tourist office in the Bonlieu centre, where bookings must also be made. The cost of a full-day excursion is 75 francs, whilst a half-day excursion costs 50 francs.

For the less energetic, the Compagnie des Bateaux à Vapeur sur le Lac Annecy operates a timetabled service around the lake, calling at most of the lakeside villages. Despite the title, the boats are alas, no longer driven by steam. They do, however, provide a lovely one-and-a-half-hour cruise, highly recommended for non-walking days or, possibly, after a walk, providing most agreeable transport back to Annecy from, say, Duingt. In addition to the timetabled service, there are round-the-lake cruises, by the principal company and by other operators. For real luxury there is the *Libellue*, rather more than a floating gin-palace, with seating for 595 and offering trips with lunch or dinner. A basic circuit of the lake costs 50–55 francs; taking lunch or dinner on the *Libellue* will add from 80 francs upwards.

Most walkers and tourists staying in or near to Annecy will wish to see something of the surrounding area in addition to, or in combination with, the walks. The following is a list of suggestions which are within easy reach by car; many are also accessible by public transport.

Rumilly   Attractive small market town.

Gorges du Fier   The river Fier is located at the bottom of a deep impressive chasm, accessible only on a walkway. The entrance charge is 19 francs.

Château de Montrottier   This is a thirteenth- to fifteenth-century château. It is very close to the Gorges du Fier, at Lovagny and also open daily in season, tel: 50 46 23 02.

Bell museum, Sévrier   This has been a bell foundry since 1796. It is a museum with video film and diaporama. It is open to visitors daily, except Mondays; on Sunday it is open in the afternoon only.

Col de Leschaux/Semnoz   The road along the spine of the Semnoz mountain is a fine excursion, returning by the Col de Leschaux. *En route* is a small animals park, an exhibition centre, and an Alpine garden.

Pont de l'Abime/Alby sur Chéran   From the Col de Leschaux, a circuit can be made by returning to Annecy on the west side of the Semnoz mountain. The bridge is a most impressive span over the river Chéran, and Alby is a sleepy medieval town with arcaded shops and of a small modern church.

La Sambuy, 2,173m (7,127ft)   Above Seythenex (near to Faverges) is the Sambuy mountain, with ascent by cable car.

Col de Tamié/Abbaye de Tamié   About 8km (5 miles) beyond Seythenex is the Col de Tamié, giving access to the valley of the Isère, south of Lake Annecy. Nearby is the beautifully situated abbey, which caters for visitors.

Duingt   Beyond the church is a 'hidden' village which is well worth finding, with narrow streets of very old houses. There are two châteaux, one jutting boldly into the lake, but neither is open to the public.

Conflans   Another amazing off-the-beaten-track survival, very close to the nondescript town of Albertville on its east side. A large village, formerly a walled city and later a market town, Conflans lost its importance in the eighteenth century and more recent history has, fortunately, passed it by. Cars must be left outside the walls.

Col de la Forclaz   The Col de la Forclaz is easily reached from the road along the east side of the lake. It is a fine viewpoint and a centre for *delta-plane* and *parapente*, varieties of hang-gliding.

Château de Menthon A fine château situated close to Menthon St Bernard (lake landing stage) and occupied by the same family since the eleventh century. Open to visitors each afternoon in July and August and on Tuesdays, Saturdays, Sundays in May, June, and September, tel: 50 60 12 05.

Thônes and La Clusaz

In order to achieve wider coverage of the area, a few of the walks are based on Thônes and La Clusaz. This gives an opportunity for walkers and tourists to become acquainted with these towns as well as enjoying different countryside.

Thônes is quite a small town, well situated at the junction of three valleys. The usual road from Annecy climbs over the Col de Bluffy with its fine views of the lake, the Château de Menthon and the Dents de Lanfon but, as a variation, it is well worth taking the road to the east of Mt Veyrier and then diverting to a minor road in the Défilé de Dingy, on the route of a Roman road. The centre of Thônes is attractive, particularly the square which has the *mairie*, the church with a *bulbe* bell tower, typical of the area, and arcaded shops. Just off the square is the tourist office, at one end of a fine sweep of public gardens and sporting facilities.

Thônes does regard itself as a winter centre, although the ski slopes and the associated lifts are some distance away. In summer it is a good walking centre, also offering: tennis, swimming, miniature golf, horse-riding, bowls, fishing, a museum, a cinema, concerts, a theatre, various fêtes, and a library. There are five hotels and 380 furnished apartments.

La Clusaz is very much a winter sports town. The town centre, clustered around the modern church is, however, more compact than is the case in many ski resorts; one particularly attractive building is the tourist office. From La Clusaz, the road up the valley to Les Confins unfolds superb views of the Aravis range of mountains, which are crossed by the Col des Aravis. Facilities at La Clusaz include swimming, tennis, mountain cycling, summer tobogganing, horse-riding, archery, golf (driving range at Les Confins), hang-gliding, and folklore festivals.

South-east Haute-Savoie

Chamonix

If there is one town in the whole of Alpine France, let alone Haute-Savoie, whose name strikes an instant response, it must be Chamonix (officially 'Chamonix Mont-Blanc'), *ville Olympique* and *capitale mondiale de l'Alpinisme*, the place where Alpine mountain climbing really began just over 200 years ago.

Dr Paccard admiring Mont Blanc, Chamonix

Unlike Annecy, Chamonix has no old town, and no important medieval buildings. Until tourism really took off, the Chamonix valley was a rural backwater, unimportant and remote, with nothing but its relatively poor farming and a priory. However, since Balmat and Paccard succeeded in climbing Mont Blanc on 8 August 1786, all that has changed and Chamonix has become a busy, bustling town, overcrowded in season, and devoted to many forms of tourism, with winter sports and summer walking and climbing paramount. As a walking centre it is a natural choice; without leaving the valley there is enough to keep enthusiasts happy for a long time. The road along the valley, together with the railway, provides a minor route into Switzerland, via the Col des Montets, and the Col de la Forclaz in the case of the road. Much more important in road communication terms is the link between France and Italy via the Mont Blanc tunnel.

Although the town is by no means beautiful, it is pleasant enough, with some good buildings such as the *mairie*. Some of the centre is pedestrianised and there are plenty of colourful pavement cafés from which the mountains can be admired. Take a seat and follow the pointing finger of Jacques Balmat, showing the way to De Saussure on their combined statue in the town centre.

Tourist accommodation of all types (for example 100 hotels and seventeen camping sites in the valley) appears to be plentiful, but could be found wanting in high season, when the ease of access along the valley brings in tourists in great numbers. There is an hotel booking service, tel: 50 55 23 33 or 50 53 00 24.

Car parking in the town centre is barely adequate, but the huge open area near the Planards restaurant and toboggan run is only 5 minutes' walk away.

A particularly good feature of the Chamonix valley is the public transport; both the railway and Chamonix bus services play an important part. The town provides every sporting facility which would be expected in a major resort, including a swimming centre with six pools, six indoor sports halls, an indoor skating rink, tennis (twenty-one courts!), golf (at Praz), summer tobogganing, horse-riding, fishing, hang-gliding, mountain cycling, mini-golf, and climbing schools (Company of Mountain Guides, Chamonix, tel: 50 54 00 12). For the less sporting there are a casino, three cinemas, an Alpine museum, musical weeks, eight nightclubs, and a Festival of Mountain Guides.

Without travelling great distances there are many good excursions, and the following are worth considering.

Col des Montets   At the head of the valley is this gentle col, with the chalet and laboratory of the Réserve Naturelle des Aiguilles Rouges and its botanical footpaths.

Argentière   This is a large village with the most attractive houses situated along the road beyond the church, which has a good baroque interior.

Le Tour   This is a village part way up the hillside beyond Argentière, almost at the foot of the glacier of the same name.

Montenvers   There is an hotel, shops, restaurant, ice cave, museum and display of rare minerals, all at more than 1,900m (6,275ft) beside and above the Mer de Glace, possibly Europe's most famous glacier. Reached in 20 minutes by the delightful Chamonix – Montenvers railway.

Les Houches   This is a large, rather straggling village with two supermarkets and a baroque church.

Merlan   Up the hill opposite Les Houches at an altitude of over 1,500m (4,920ft), is this 23-hectare (55-acre) animal reserve. Open to the public daily in season, charging (adults) 10 francs and (children) 5 francs.

Servoz   A few kilometres further down the valley, noted for the Gorges de la Diosaz (walkway access only, open to visitors in season, charging (adults) 15 francs), the Museum of Alpine Fauna, and a baroque church.

Plateau d'Assy   Up the hillside above Passy is this large, scattered village, with the modern church of Notre Dame de Toutes-Grâces, designed by the architect Novarina, well known in Thonon and Evian, and decorated by no less than Chagall, Léger, Rouault, Matisse, Lurçat, and Richier. There is also the exquisite little lake, Lac Vert, which can also be reached on foot from Servoz.

St Gervais les Bains   In part, quite a pleasant town with a thermal establishment in a large park down the hill at Le Fayet. St Gervais itself has a good range of facilities with sport being prominent. The main church is baroque, but perhaps more unusual is the modern church of Notre Dame des Alpes. Most important is the Tramway de Mont Blanc, a rack railway starting opposite the SNCF station in Le Fayet, climbing to St Gervais and continuing for about 13km (8 miles) to its summit at Nid de l'Aigle (Eagle's Nest), at a height of nearly 2,400m (7,826 ft), and close to the Bionnassy glacier in the Mont Blanc massif. There are intermediate stations and the potential for walkers is immense. A one-way journey from end to end takes $1^1/_4$ hours and a return trip costs about £9 (tel: 50 78 27 23).

Megève   Yet another holiday resort with a golf course and a full range of other sporting facilities. Mt D'Arbois, reached by cable lift, is a particularly good viewpoint for Mont Blanc.

Les Contamines-Montjoie   A village in the valley to the south of St Gervais les Bains, with a baroque church having a *bulbe* bell tower and a notable retable. Further up the valley, almost at the end of the road, is the chapel of Notre Dame de la Gorge.

Aiguille du Midi Cable lifts abound in the Chamonix valley and are available either as excursions in their own right or as an aid to walkers in reaching areas not otherwise readily accessible. A list is included in the general information chapter. The lift which reaches Aiguille du Midi does, however, warrant special consideration for several reasons. Firstly it reaches an altitude of 3,842m (12,602ft), and is the highest cable car in Europe. Secondly, the Aiguille is not otherwise accessible to walkers. Thirdly, in the construction of the lift, records for the longest unsupported length of cable and the highest above the ground – 500m (1,640ft) – were broken. Fourthly, there are connections with other lifts which enable Courmayeur on the Italian side of Mont Blanc to be reached via La Pointe Helbronner. The total one-way journey takes not less than $1^1/_2$ hours and something like 4 hours would need to be allowed for the whole excursion. It is, inevitably, expensive. Chamonix to the Aiguille and return costs 114 francs (£12), whilst Chamonix to Pte. Helbronner and return costs 174 francs (£18). It goes without saying that the views are breathtaking.

East/Central Haute-Savoie

The east/central part of Haute-Savoie does not have a natural base town such as Annecy in the south-west or Chamonix in the south-east. However, there is good walking country and much of interest for the visitor. The walks in this area are reachable by driving from Chamonix, but if you prefer to spend less of your time in a car, Morzine, Samoëns and Taninges are recommended as the most likely choices for a base in this part of the *département*.

Morzine

Morzine is the biggest of the three towns and, as a major winter sports centre (with its high-level offshoot Avoriaz), is the best equipped in terms of hotels, apartments and shops.

The town is situated immediately to the east of the Cluses to Thonon les Bains road, 19km (12 miles) north of Taninges, straggling somewhat along the valley of the river Dranse, with its *centre* very much at one end. Road access to Morzine is only fair; the Cluses to Thonon road is winding and narrow for much of its length and the motorway access at Cluses is 30km (19 miles) distant, as is the nearest railway station, also at Cluses.

The town itself is unashamedly a holiday resort, which can be a good or a bad thing, depending on the viewpoint. On the good side it means a general appreciation of the needs of holiday makers, particularly with regard to accommodation, to sport and to other leisure activities. It means that the town is kept clean and smart, and well provided with floral decorations. Unfortunately, it also means that there are few buildings of any interest other than the nineteenth-century church, no 'old French town' atmosphere, a plethora of winter sports equipment shops and a very dead feel to the town out of season. The impressive range of facilities includes indoor ice skating and ice hockey, swimming, hang-gliding and parachute gliding, tennis (thirteen courts), horse-riding, rock-climbing instruction, mountain cycling, canoeing (inflatable craft), golf (driving range), fishing, bowls and two cinemas. Many of the sporting facilities are offered with instructional courses for adults and children. There is also a comprehensive programme of events throughout the summer – concerts, fêtes of all descriptions and a one-week musical course.

Surprisingly, there is only one camping site. Suggested excursions from Morzine include the following.

Bellevaux   A village in the Brévon valley with an attractive nineteenth-century church – *bulbe* bell tower, paintings and furniture. Reached from Morzine by a tortuous route via Le Jotty and Vailly.

Lac de Vallon   From Bellevaux, continue up the valley to reach Lac de Vallon, created by a landslide in 1943, St Bruno chapel and the fine view of the Roc d'Enfer.

Risse Valley/Verte Valley   From the Brévon Valley, the Risse Valley and the Verte Valley are reached by the Col de Jambaz in the first case and then by the Col de Terramont. A return from the Verte valley may be made by way of the Col des Arces to Lulin and Vailly.

Gorges du Pont du Diable   At Le Jotty on the main Cluses to Thonon-les-Bains road are the Gorges du Pont du Diable, where the river Dranse flows through a deep narrow defile. It is open daily for visitors (in season).

St Jean d'Aulps   A large village situated on the main road 8km (5 miles) north of Morzine. The village church is nineteenth-century, but the main interest is the ruin of a twelfth-century abbey.

Montriond   A modest village with a baroque church, but most famous for its lake, approximately 3km (2 miles) beyond (*see* Walk 20(b)). La Cascade d'Ardent, an impressive waterfall, is a little further along the road leading to Les Lindarets.

Les Lindarets   'The village of the goats', a noted cheese-producing community high up the valley. It is possible to complete a circuit by returning to Morzine over the Col de la Joux Verte.

Avoriaz A notable ski resort, famous for its contemporary architecture in wood and for its lake and general mountain views.

Pointe de Nyon 2,020m (6,626ft) This excellent viewpoint above Morzine is accessible by cable-lift.

Ardoisières and Manche Two pleasant valleys rising comparatively gently from Morzine.

Samoëns

Like Morzine, Samoëns, coupled with its high-level ski resort of Samoëns 1600, is a holiday town. It does, however, have more of the feel of a real market town and the centre is a pleasant jumble of old buildings in small streets. Access by road is reasonably good; 21km (13 miles) to the motorway at Cluses, over half of the distance being on a good, straight road to Taninges. The nearest railway station is also at Cluses. There is no shortage of accommodation for visitors, with twelve hotels and plenty of apartments, but only one camping site.

Within Samoëns, the church, with modern stained glass, and the Alpine garden of Jaÿsinia are most interesting. The latter is impressive, with apparently endless terracing above the town and with superb views of the Criou mountain, which dominates Samoëns. The range of plants displayed is comprehensive and a stream descends in a series of waterfalls. The town has a good range of shops and the leisure facilities are excellent, with a cinema, a library, a sauna, a leisure park with archery, canoeing, fishing, tennis (eight courts), swimming, hang-gliding, horse-riding, volleyball, mini-golf, golf (driving range) and cross-country cycling. There are also guided tours of the town on three days each week in season, guided mountain walks and instruction in rock climbing. Fêtes, concerts and special events take place during the summer, many of them associated with the Alpine garden.

The following are some suggested excursions.

Sixt A large and attractive village with a former abbey and twelfth/thirteenth-century church with *bulbe* bell tower and seventeenth-century refectory.

Fer à Cheval The road past Sixt ends at the magnificent Fer à Cheval cirque of mountains, with the Tenneverge 2,987m (9,558ft) dominant, and several waterfalls in view. At the end of the road is a restaurant/bar, a natural history exhibition centre, and a huge area for picnics and informal rambling in woodland.

Cascade du Rouget   A right turn at Sixt towards Maison Neuve and Salvagny leads to this celebrated waterfall.

Gorge de Tines   About a mile before reaching Sixt, to the right of the road the river Giffre runs in a deep narrow channel, spanned by a footbridge (*see* Walk 21).

Les Allamands   Valley immediately to the north from Samoëns. The road peters out in about 8km (5 miles).

Col de Joux Plane   The minor road linking Samoëns and Morzine climbs over 1,700m (5,576ft) and is not open in winter. Near the top is a small lake and a bar/restaurant.

Verchaix   Along the main road to Taninges is Verchaix Gare, the station, unfortunately, having long been disused. There are restaurants and a camping site. Up a short, sharp hill is Verchaix itself, a tiny village clustered around its church and with good views over the Giffre valley.

Taninges

On the face of it, Taninges is the least likely of the three towns for use as a walking or touring base. It is not really a holiday town and the facilities for visitors do not compare with those at Morzine and Samoëns. Having said that, Taninges does have certain advantages. Its road and rail access are the best of the three; 10km (6 miles) to the motorway and railway station at Cluses, and its own direct road to Geneva,

The town itself has some historic buildings, most within a small 'old town' and there is life induced by a weekly market. The nineteenth-century church is the largest in the Annecy diocese, whilst close by is the thirteenth-century Chapelle de Flérier. The former chapel of St Anne in the old quarter is now a house, but has retained its old *bulbe* bell tower. On the eastern fringe of the town is the Mélan church, which is thirteenth-century, with a sixteenth-century cloister.

Hotels, apartments, and restaurants are rather lacking in Taninges, but the shops, including a supermarket, are adequate. There is only one camping site, but it does stay open all the year round and is well managed by the local council. Organised attractions include tennis, gymnastics, watersports, fishing, exhibitions, concerts and the occasional fête.

Possible excursions can include the following.

Le Praz de Lys   At 1,500m (4,920ft) this scattered ski resort is the 'other half' of Taninges. Set on a plateau, it is easily reached via the Pont des Gets. Good mountain scenery and rambles (*see* Walk 20(a) for Lac de Roy). A return to Taninges by the Col de la Ramaz, Messy, and Mieussy completes the circuit.

Les Gets   A sizeable winter sports centre on the main Taninges to Morzine road. The church has modern tapestry and there is a museum of mechanical music. Mt Chéry may be ascended by cable-lift for wide-ranging views.

Cluses   There have already been many references to Cluses as the centre of communications in this part of Haute-Savoie. It is a sizeable town, with all the essential facilities, and clearly its use as a base merits serious consideration. However, the town has expanded rapidly during the past few years. Its traditional watch and clock making has become large-scale precision engineering, and vast areas of the valley towards Bonneville have become industrial, commercial and residential suburbs. This valley also carries the railway, the motorway and the original main road. For these reasons it is suggested that most walkers and tourists would prefer not to stay in the valley of the river Arve, and would want to visit Cluses only on a sightseeing and shopping basis.

Bonneville   About 15km (10 miles) down the valley from Cluses. Quite a pleasant old town, but positioned rather close to all the bustle of the Arve valley. It has a château, museum, arcaded shops and an old wooden bell tower.

Viuz-en-Sallaz   About 20km (13 miles) along the direct road from Taninges to Geneva is the country life museum of Viuz; it is open daily (except Monday) throughout the year, tel: 50 36 89 18.

Northern Haute-Savoie

The northern boundary of much of Haute-Savoie is the southern shore of Lac Léman. The fringe of the Alps reaches the lake near St Gingolph on the Swiss frontier, but the mountains are set back a few kilometres behind Evian and Thonon. The country, known as Chablais, between mountains and lake is comparatively gentle, and is dotted with agricultural and residential villages. The lake shore itself is quite intensively developed, with the two towns and many villages, merging together in places.

The climate is a little softer than among the mountains, possibly due to a tempering effect from the large body of water, coupled with the lower altitude. On the whole, this northern part of Haute-Savoie offers a good range and variety of walking, some of which can be more gentle than is the case further south. The Léman Littoral path runs along, or close to, the shoreline for a considerable distance. Further inland and generally at a fairly high level is the Balcon du Léman. Both these long distance routes feature in part in the recommended walks. Within easy reach is the Abondance valley and its various offshoots, providing higher and tougher mountain walking.

The choice of a base depends, firstly, on whether or not proximity to the lake and town facilities is of importance. If so, then it must be Evian, Thonon, or one of the adjacent villages. If not, then Abondance warrants serious consideration.

Access to both Thonon and Evian is reasonably good, by rail along the branch line from Geneva/Annemasse or by road from the motorway system (Annemasse exit), a distance of 34km (21 miles) to Thonon and a further 9km (6 miles) to Evian. Those travelling by roads other than motorways will approach either via Geneva and the RN5, or Bellegarde–Annemasse (RN206/D903). Abondance is a little less easy to reach. Any of the recommended routes may be used as far as Thonon, then the way is to the right up the valley of the river Dranse (D903) for 11km (7 miles) to the left turn into the Abondance valley (D22). Abondance is a further 15km ($9^1/_2$ miles) along the valley.

Thonon les Bains

Thonon is a fair-sized town rising high above the lake shore. The town is linked with its port (Rives) by a funicular railway descending among the floral terraces. It is a lively place, with good partially pedestrianised shopping areas, squares, and pavement cafés. The many old buildings are a reminder of an important historic past – the Château de Bellegarde, now the courthouse, the Château de Sonnaz, now the Chablais museum, the Château de Montjoux, at the port, the huge, oddly shaped church of St Hippolyte, with its twelfth-century crypt, and the Chapelle de l'Ancienne Visitation, used for exhibitions.

In more recent times, Thonon has acquired fame as a thermal spa, which accounts for the generous provision of hotels and apartments in and close to the town. This accommodation is now supplemented by several camping sites; the one at St Disdille has places for over 600 tents or caravans. Despite the continuing popularity of its mineral water, Thonon's attraction as a spa has obviously faded or, perhaps, been overtaken by events. However, the town is clearly not attempting to live on its former glories, as there is no lack of interesting modern buildings such as the Maison des Arts et Loisirs (architect Novarina) and the nearby fountain. In the suburb of Vongy, by the side of the main road, is the church of Notre Dame du Léman (Novarina again), whilst other twentieth-century churches are Notre Dame de Lourdes on the Avenue Général de Gaulle at Morcy and Notre Dame des Vallées to the south of the town centre at Tully. Back in the town centre there is some interesting contemporary development close to the tourist office, which itself shares part of a lovely old former convent with the library.

The lakeside has the port, a pleasure boat marina, and a long, seaside-like promenade, the Quai de Ripaille, which leads to the municipal beach and swimming pool and to the Château de Ripaille (*see* Walk 29(a)) a large wine-producing and woodland estate based on a fifteenth-century château.

Local bus services are centred on a spacious bus station in the Place des Arts, a large square close to the railway station. Other local transport is by water, and there is a regular service from the port linking all the main towns and some villages around the lake.

In the town centre, car parking is restricted and must be paid for. The spacious parking areas at the port are better for a longer stay, using the funicular to climb to the town or enjoying the short, steep walk either through the gardens or by an attractive street with old houses. Thonon has all the sporting and leisure facilities which would be expected in a holiday town. There is particular emphasis on watersports, but tennis, horse-riding, archery, accompanied walks and many more are all available, as are two cinemas (five screens), several art galleries, a library, two museums, bridge, scrabble and tarot clubs, discothèques, nightclubs, and various festivals. There is a good hypermarket on the eastern fringe of the town.

Evian les Bains

Evian is only about half the size of Thonon but its fame as a thermal spa and, above all, the popularity of its mineral water, have made its name a household word internationally. As at Thonon, there is a port and a long lakeside promenade (this one backed by the busy RN5 main road). As a whole, the town, with its largely pedestrianised rue National main street, seems to be less lively than Thonon, but it is by no means unattractive. There are well-tended public gardens in abundance and the thermal spa is still important, as evidenced by the replacement of the grand old building by a modern *buvette* (the architect was once again Novarina) at the eastern end of the town.

The *hôtel de ville*, with its copy of Rodin's *Thinker*, is one of many good buildings along the lake frontage, including the casino, which has a style all of its own. A little further west is the large church, with wall paintings, and the tourist office, which is part of a rather stylish modern development. In the main street is the former *hôtel de ville* (dating from the fifteenth to nineteenth-centuries) and the impressive headquarters of the Cachat mineral water organisation (built in 1900).

As would be expected, there is no lack of holiday accommodation. From the splendours of the Royal Hotel, perched above the town, to the most humble of camping sites, most visitors will find something for their needs.

Local transport is good for a comparatively small town, two bus services giving good coverage from the Gare Routière, very centrally situated. On the lake, the Evian port has the regular service to the other ports, the direct service across to Lausanne being particularly good.

Sporting and leisure facilities are comprehensive including the Royal Golf Club (tel: 50 75 14 00) with pitch and putt and putting green, the Royal Tennis Club, plenty of watersports, cinema, casino, library and discothèques. Accompanied mountain walks are available; enquiries should be made at the tourist office.

Abondance

Abondance is an entirely different kind of base for a walking holiday in northern Haute-Savoie, comprising an old village around a big square and with a famous former abbey beside the main road. It is situated half-way along the valley of the same name, among good mountains and traditional Alpine agriculture, the chalets of the valley being particularly famous, as is the Abondance breed of dairy cattle and the local variety of Tomme cheese. Winter sport is paramount further up the valley towards Châtel, but Abondance itself has only two lifts and is not entirely given over to tourism. It is quite an attractive village and the amount of accommodation is good for its size. It has seven hotels, 300 furnished apartments and one camping site, open all the year. About 6km (4 miles) along the valley at La Chapelle d'Abondance is another village of comparative size and facilities.

Local transport comprises bus services up and down the valley; by car, communication with the main road (D902) in the Dranse valley is good and the route to Evian via Chevenoz is also easy. A little more adventurous is the road over the Col du Corbier to Le Biot and Morzine, whilst the Pas de Morgins above Châtel crosses the frontier into Switzerland.

In the village is the great thirteenth-century abbatical church combined with the former fifteenth-century abbey. The latter has a fourteenth-century cloister with very important fifteenth-century frescoes by Giacomo Jaquierio, and there is also a museum of religious apparel and ornaments. Inevitably, the facilities for visitors cannot compare with those at Thonon or Evian and there is no lake, but for many walkers the mountain surroundings and the slightly easier access to some of the walks will more than compensate. Fishing, guided walks, botanical excursions, tennis, archery, mountain cycling, visits to a cheese-making dairy and a taxidermist's workshop(!) are all offered. There are also occasional concerts and, annually in August, a great church/abbey festival.

The following is a list of excursions from all three centres.

Gorges du Diable   *See under* Morzine.

St Jean d'Aulps   *See under* Morzine.

Yvoire   This medieval walled town is a remarkable survival, and is situated on the edge of the lake.

Excevenex   Said to have the best beach on Lac Léman; a good stretch of fine sand, backed by a camping and caravan site.

Sciez and Séchex   These are small harbours with bars, restaurants and camping sites.

St Gingolph   A port and small town on the Swiss frontier.

Bernex   A large, scattered village and winter sports centre, sitting below the Dent d'Oche mountain and the much lower Mt César. It has an interesting church.

Lac de la Beunaz   This small, privately-owned lake, 2km ($1^1/_2$ miles) on the Evian side of Bernex, is well equipped as a bathing centre.

Châtel   A winter sports centre and summer holiday resort, close to the Swiss frontier at Pas de Morgins. The Essert waterfall is 5km (3 miles) further up the valley.

Vacheresse   Noted cheese-producing village.

Chalets de Bise   The hamlet of Bise is situated at the end of a long steep minor road, that leaves the Abondance valley just above Vacheresse. It is right at the foot of the impressive Cornettes de Bise 2,432m (7,976ft). At the hamlet is a refuge, horses roaming wild, and a sizeable lake, the bed of which is generally dry. Another, similar, lake is Lac Léchère, 2km ($1^1/_4$ miles) back down the road and not too easy to find. However, right by the roadside is a much smaller lake, very prettily situated, and guaranteed to have water. At a junction 3km (2 miles) below this little lake is a road fork to Ubine (*see* Walk 25), with its chapel and refuge. From the roadside close to the junction, the tiny Chapelle de la Paraz has an apparently impossible situation, clinging high on the cliff face opposite.

La Chapelle d'Abondance   A winter sports and tourist village close to Abondance. It has a baroque church with *bulbe* bell tower.

Geneva   An obvious excursion for major shopping, museums and galleries. Accessible by rail (though subject to a rather awkward timetable), and bus (1 hour from Thonon), or car.

Lausanne   Good boat service across the lake, 35 minutes from Evian.

THE WALKS

Walk 1   Annecy: The Abandoned Mine

Map no:	IGN 1:50,000: 2; Bornes-Bauges
Walking time:	3 hours
Grading:	Moderate with good paths but one long steady climb
Ascent:	550m (1,804ft)
Highest altitude:	1,050m (3,444ft)
Lowest altitude:	500m (1,640ft)

A walk including a great deal of attractive mixed woodland with some industrial archaeology interest.

From Annecy take the main road to Albertville (N508). At Bout du Lac turn right on to a minor road signposted to Lathuile (D180). Park cars in Lathuile village by the *Mairie*.

The Walk

Leave Lathuile village by the road signposted to 'Saurie 2', noting also a fingerpost indicating the walk to the abandoned mine. The route is marked throughout by green triangles. After a short distance fork left by a tree with a green triangle. In 150m, just before passing a farm on the left, fork right. This stony track is the start of the old road to the mine, marked by both red and white bands and the familiar green triangle. It is also part of no less than three long-distance footpaths – GR96, Tour du Lac d'Annecy, and Grande

50

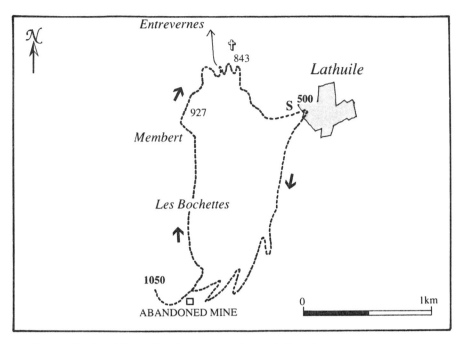

Traversée des Alpes. To the music of cow bells, the ascent commences, continuing all the way to the old mine at a ruling gradient of about 1 in 7. Before entering the woodland you will see a shapely wooded peak ahead. Look out for large stones on the track which have been deeply grooved by the wheels of the mine traffic and, at the same time, admire the skill of the miners who constructed such an excellent road traversing a steep and difficult mountainside. Spare a thought also for the horses, who must have had a hard working life hauling empty wagons up such a gradient.

Occasional gaps in the trees allow glimpses of the valley below and of the mountains on the east side of the lake, La Tournette inevitably being prominent. Red and white markings on rocks and trees give periodic reassurance of the route, which is quite straightforward. Superficially the workings of the long-abandoned coal mine are disappointing, but there may well be interesting discoveries for the more adventurous. However, the setting is dramatic with a sharp peak towering several hundred feet above.

Leave the mine by the track rising to the right, signposted 'Entrevernes' and cross high pastures, coloured with crocuses in autumn, with a marvellous view down into the valley as the highest point on the route is reached.

Shortly after passing a farm building, bear right, following the green triangles, soon reaching a metalled road. About 800m (875yds) before the village of Entrevernes, turn right into a track signposted 'Belvédère. Lathuile' and also 'Site de l'Oratoire – 5 minutes'. The Oratoire is a small shrine and the belvedere is a superb viewpoint close by. The inclined platform is a take off point for paragliding and hang-gliding, popular sports in this area.

Set off on the last lap down a path to the right, signposted 'Lathuile' and forecasting 45 minutes walking time. The path is initially steep and stony. It soon improves underfoot but continues downhill at an angle which many walkers may find to be a little uncomfortable, virtually all the way to Lathuile. Turn right in the village to return to the *Mairie*.

The old town, Annecy

Walk 2   Annecy: Tour du Roc de Chère

Map no:	IGN 1:50,000: 2; Bornes-Bauges
Walking time:	$1^1/_2$ – 2 hours
Grading:	Easy
Ascent:	Very little
Highest altitude:	610m (2,001ft)
Lowest altitude:	559m (1,834ft)

A short, comparatively gentle stroll with an extra $^1/_2$ hour if the optional diversion is added. There is very little ascent on the main circuit, but one downhill section is rather steep and may be slippery following rain.

From Annecy take the road along the east side of the lake, towards Talloires. After passing Echarvines take the first turning on the right, leading to the Golf du Lac d'Annecy. Cars may be parked at the golf club.

The Walk

Walk back from the car park to a large board which sets out various walks on the Roc de Chère. Follow the adjacent footpath signposted 'Tour du Roc de Chère', and at the first junction fork right, skirting the edge of the golf course, and then climb steadily but gently to the left, looking for yellow marks on rocks and trees. For most of this walk, the route is in woodland, in this case generally deciduous, with oak and birch prominent. On reaching a junction look for wooden signs set high on trees, and bear left following the 'Talloires. Belvédère' sign, shortly reaching a board marking the entrance to a nature reserve. The belvedere is reached a little further to the right.

This viewpoint is a rocky outcrop, flanked with heather, and with wide-ranging views over the upper part of Lake Annecy, Duingt village with its châteaux, and the great ridge rising behind.

To continue the walk, face the lake from behind the rocks and look for a narrow footpath to the left descending steeply, with red marks on a rock on the left-hand side. The path continues to drop, winding amongst the trees,

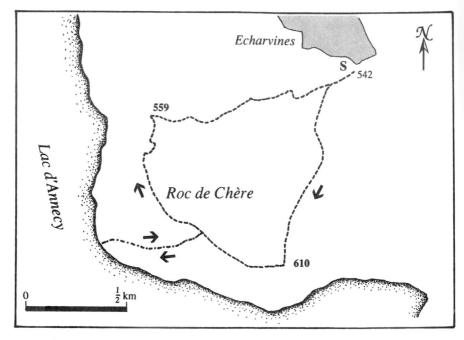

with occasional red markings to confirm the route. When the gradient eases, the track widens and becomes an attractive woodland ramble, bearing steadily to the right. You will then reach a clearing, with paths to left and right; carry straight on, and in little more than 50m the start of the optional diversion to the shore of the lake is apparent on the left. This is a narrower path, marked by white bands on the trees. The descent to the lake is considerable and $^1/_2$ hour extra walking time should be allowed, the majority being for the ascending return journey.

The main path continues to a crossing; turn right here and then bear left, still following the familiar red signs. The golf course is soon reached and the path now skirts one of the greens, before following the edge of a fairway back towards the club house and the car park. High-velocity golf balls are a potential danger and French golfers may or may not shout 'fore!' intelligibly – take no chances; evasive action is advised on hearing any shout whatsoever! The view is excellent, with the Château du Menthon prominent below Mt Baron. This château is open to the public, the hours varying according to the season.

Walk 3　Annecy: Duingt and the Taillefer Ridge

Map no:	IGN 1:50,000: 2; Bornes-Bauges
Walking time:	$3^1/_2$ – 4 hours
Grading:	Moderate with some safe scrambling.
Ascent:	318m (1,043ft)
Highest altitude:	765m (2,509ft)
Lowest altitude:	447m (1,466ft)

This walk involves 318m (1,043ft) in ascending the Taillefer ridge, in places necessitating scrambling on rock. The scrambling is easy and always safe despite the generally sheer sides of the ridge. A shorter version , of about 2 hours, is possible.

Duingt village is approximately $14^1/_2$km (9 miles) from Annecy, along the lakeside road (N508). Turn right by the church and park either in the large open area, or in the marked parking place alongside the cycle track, which is a disused railway line, complete with tunnel.

The Walk

Walk away from the church towards the main part of the village. In less than 50m there is an obvious path on the right, with many signposts including 'Grotte de Notre Dame du Lac' and 'Belvédère St Michel'. Proceed upwards, climbing the steep end of the Taillefer ridge. This first section is furnished with the Stations of the Cross in preparation for arrival at the Grotte de Notre Dame du Lac, an impressive grotto, floodlit after dark, and with a terrace which provides a viewpoint for the northern part of the lake. Retrace the route for about 30m and take a narrow footpath rising to the right. Red and yellow markings will be seen on a tree and a signpost 'Sentier du Taillefer – 765 metres'. You will then reach a fine statue of St Michael. The path continues upwards and many of the trees carry identification labels. It is interesting to spot these and to see how many you know, either by recognition or by translation from the French or (for the informed botanists) the Latin

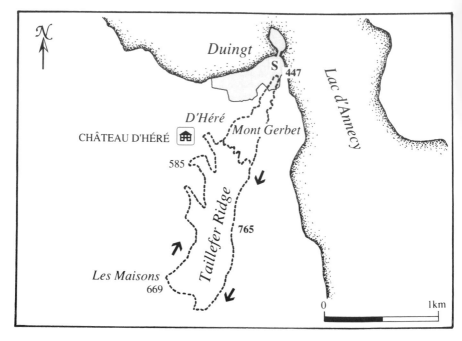

names. Included are *pin de Corse; charme; noisetier commun; pin sylvestre; chêne pubescent; peuplier tremble; châtaignier; alisier blanc*. At an intersection turn right, reassured by red and yellow markings on a tree. The path keeps close to the crest of the ridge, rising steadily. The toil is rewarded by glimpses of the lake on both sides, despite the thick woodland. The Dent du Lanfon and the wooded mound of the Roc de Chère (the location of Walk 2), are prominent. At a small clearing, provided with two seats, follow a signpost towards 'Entrevernes – 1^1/$_2$ hours'.

At a junction look carefully for red and yellow signs combined and bear left uphill. The going becomes steep and stony, but is unlikely to trouble walkers familiar with, say, hill walking in the Lake District or North Wales. A small bridge with a handrail facilitates the passage above a precipice.

The summit of the Taillefer 765m (2,510ft), a distinct hump on the continuous ridge, is soon reached. Carry on through a patch of heather and, where forward progress would be fatal, turn sharply right to avoid a quarry which bites deeply into the ridge.

The hamlet of Les Maisons is below to the right and the path is now losing height steadily. At the next junction turn right to descend more steeply to a small meadow. Just before reaching the meadow, turn right again, along the bottom fringe of the woodland, the path here being very indistinct. Another meadow is reached; keep to the left and cross the stream by a wooden farm bridge, heading for the farm buildings where the road is reached. Turn right and walk back to Duingt along a very scenic and little-used road. At the Château d'Héré, a right turn into an even more minor road provides the shortest return route.

The shorter version of this walk necessitates finding a right turn well before the Taillefer summit, aiming for the D'Héré hamlet. Before reaching the hamlet, take a lane on the right at a farm, which goes behind the buildings, and then reaches the very minor road leading to Duingt.

Either before or after the walk, try to visit the old part of Duingt village, hidden below the ridge, and fortunately missed by most of the tourists rushing up and down the lakeside road. It is a gem of old world France, to be enjoyed only on foot.

Walk 4   Annecy: Tour des Rochers des Becs

Map no:	IGN 1:50,000: 2; Bornes-Bauges
Walking time:	$2^1/_2$ hours
Grading:	Easy
Ascent:	290m (951ft)
Highest altitude:	828m (2,716ft)
Lowest altitude:	538m (1,765ft)

The Annecy end of the Semnoz mountain provides a multitude of forest trails, very close indeed to the town. The going is always easy underfoot on this walk. As virtually all the trails have names and coloured markings, the description of the route is inevitably very complex. However, missing the route is likely to be of little real consequence; the walker is seldom far from the Semnoz road (D41) and a return to base should pose no real difficulty.

From Annecy take the Albertville road (N508), turning right into the Semnoz road (D41) at the crest of a rise a little before the hospital entrance. In a short distance the Belvédère camping site is reached on the right. Cars are parked just beyond this camp at Carrefour du Gaillard, where there is a large plan of the various tracks on this end of the mountain.

The Walk

The first objective is a red marked route – the 'Circuit des Crêtes' (suggested time 2 hours 30 minutes). Head into the forest and climb steeply to the right to cross a road. Following a large red arrow on a tree, continue until the road is met again. Cross directly into a narrower track, cutting off a large loop in the road.

Take the track signposted 'Auberge de Jeunesse', and now carrying the title 'Chemin des Dames'. The way carries on through the forest of tall pines; when you reach a barrier, carry straight on. Very shortly, turn up to the right, following a signpost 'La Grande Jeanne'. Continue following the red markings, and you will shortly reach the 'Rond-point de Bellevue Alt. 640 metres',

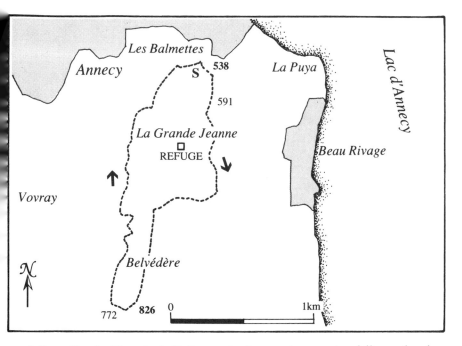

followed by the Chemin de Bellevue. At the next intersection follow red and yellow triangles to the left and carry straight on at a sign for 'Chemin du Belvédère'.

On the right is a large boulder, signposted 'Bloc Erratique'. Turn right at the sign 'Sentier de la Combe Noire' and ascend to cross the D41 road yet again, proceeding by a track with an *attention au feu* sign. Turn left at an intersection at the top of a steep section, following red and yellow signs.

At the sign 'Sentier des Ramiers', turn left and after about 60m turn right, again following the red signs, into the 'Sentier Louis Lachat'. Fork right, rising slightly, to keep the road below on the left. Go straight on at the next junction and, as the main track bends left towards the road, look carefully for a minor track on the right, the 'Sentier des Fayards'.

Keep following the red markings, straight on at the next three intersections, keeping the road below on the left. Head up to the right, to Sentier des Bruyères, turn sharp right at Sentier de la Crête (red triangle), and follow a much narrower but very attractive path. In less than 5 minutes the crest is reached. This is a remarkable viewpoint, with facing seats and a sign 'Alt. 828m'. The Vovray industrial area of Annecy lies at its feet and there are long views in several directions.

Continue in the same direction with steep cliffs below on the left, turn left at Sentier des Chanterelles, and walk as far as the Belvédère des Gélinottes, then straight on along the ridge, turning left at the sign 'Cairn Alt. 769m'.

On reaching Rond-point des Ecureuils – a circle of stones around a tree – turn sharp left into the Chemin Dessus les Becs and follow yellow signs, bearing right at Sentier des Rochers and carrying on past Sentier des Fougères. Note white signs in addition to the yellow. Turn right at a junction, pass the sign 'Chemin Sous les Becs', at the next junction fork right (yellow triangle) and reach a plaque in honour of A. Ernest Guinier, Inspector of Forests for Annecy for ten years. Turn left immediately after the plaque and bear left down a track with red and white markings to reach a road at a car parking place. This is the Carrefour de la Tambourne. Take the road to the right, then the middle of three roads at a junction, to return to the Carrefour de Gaillard in a further 100m.

Walk 5 Annecy (Thônes): Forest Circuit

Map no:	IGN 1:50,000: 2; Bornes-Bauges
Walking time:	2 hours
Grading:	Moderate to easy
Ascent:	280m (918ft)
Highest altitude:	907m (2,975ft)
Lowest altitude:	627m (2,057ft)

Thônes is a small market town, 20km (13 miles) from Annecy by the D16/ D909 roads. Its situation among the mountains, at the junction of three valleys, makes it a good centre for walking. The town is very pleasant, with arcaded shops and restaurants and there is a generous amount of town centre car parking.

There are excellent tracks throughout this moderately easy walk although one or two short sections could be slippery after rain. Although much of the route is in woodland, there are views for most of the time.

The Walk

Start walking from the square (Place de la Mairie) along the covered passage (Passage des Addebouts) towards the cinema. Cross a street and follow the Chemin du Mont rising towards the forest. On reaching the forest, there is a comprehensive guide post. The selected route is basically No. 2 entitled the 'Circuit du Reservoir', sharing a track with No. 1 for some distance.

This broad track is well graded and gains height steadily. Look out for notices on the trees giving species and planting dates; for example, *Epicéas – plantés de 1923 à 1927; Mélèzes – plantés en 1865; plantation 1979 – Epicéas, Mélèzes, Douglas.*

At a prominent junction, continue rising to the right and, at the second zigzag, note blue and red arrows on a rock. Very shortly after the second zigzag take a short diversion to the left, signposted 'table rond' to reach a clearing in the wood.

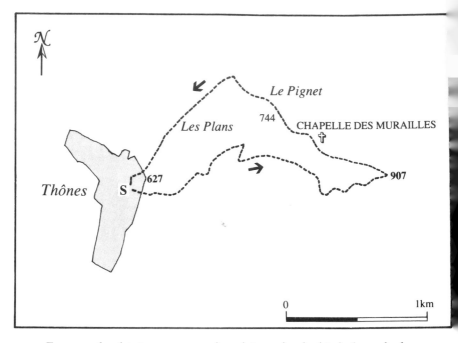

Fortunately, this is not yet another claim to be the birthplace, the home, or the place of death of the much travelled King Arthur. Cornwall and Brittany can carry on unchallenged with their Celtic legend and Camelot can remain wherever the most recent expert opinion decrees. This round table is a very modest picnic table which would certainly not accommodate anything like twenty-four knights! The clearing is, however, distinguished by a quotation from A. Theuriea: 'Au plus profond des bois, la patrie a son coeur; un peuple sans forêt est un peuple qui meurt' (in the deepest woodland, the nation has its heart, a nation without forest is a nation which is dying).

Rejoin the track, still with red and white markings, where quiet walkers may be rewarded by hearing a woodpecker at work. At a junction of paths, with an abundance of signs, go straight ahead following Circuit du Réservoir which is locally No. 2. In just over 200m take the lower path, again signposted. Cross the headwaters of a small stream (Nant Corbeau), then another stream, the track having become a narrow but still very well-defined footpath. Nant Bruyant is soon reached. This is a stream with a footbridge in an attractive gorge.

Cross another bridge and, at a 'Circuit du Réservoir' sign, carry straight on along a narrow path clinging to the valley side and steadily descending. At a fork bear right, slightly uphill, following a sign 'Chapelle – 100m'. This is

The Bridge at Nant Bruyant

the Chapelle des Murailles, which is a small but attractive shrine.

Continue in the same direction to reach an unsurfaced road in a short distance. Turn left and descend towards Thônes. This road, the Chemin des Murailles, soon becomes tarmac surfaced, but is still pleasant to walk on, being largely traffic free and winding among Alpine chalets. Left turns on to more important roads complete the return to the main town square.

Walk 6 Annecy: La Tournette 2,352m (7,713ft)

Map no:	IGN 1:50,000: 2; Bornes-Bauges
Walking time:	7 hours
Grading:	Experienced with some mountain walking
Ascent:	1,282m (4,206ft)
Highest altitude:	2,352m (7,713ft)
Lowest altitude:	1,150m (3,680ft)

This is purely and simply the ascent of a mountain and will appeal only to those walkers who have experienced, and presumably enjoyed, mountain walking in the UK.

La Tournette is a great rocky mass, dominating the upper part of Annecy lake and, to walkers who do not climb rocks, its visible face looks impregnable. However, it is a major part of the view from so many of the walks in the Annecy area that many with red blood in their veins will want to climb this highest local mountain 'because it's there'. This is a long and rather tiring climb; however, the time and effort may be reduced by using a different starting place.

From Annecy take the road along the east side of the lake through Veyrier du Lac and Menthon St Bernard (D909). Fork left before Talloires on to the road to the Col de la Forclaz (D42). Park at the col, which is equipped with several snack bars, gift shops, and a reasonable amount of parking space. It does, however, become crowded in high season particularly at weekends. A useful alternative is to carry on over the col, taking a left fork to the Chalet de l'Aulp just before reaching Montmin. Where the road surfacing ends, there is room to park several cars. The ascent from here is 1,136m (3,727ft). Those who care less for their cars than for their feet and their leg muscles can continue to drive up the stony road, reaching the Col de l'Aulp, where there is a refreshment châlet and the ascent is now reduced to 928m (3,044 ft); the time needed can also be reduced by at least one hour.

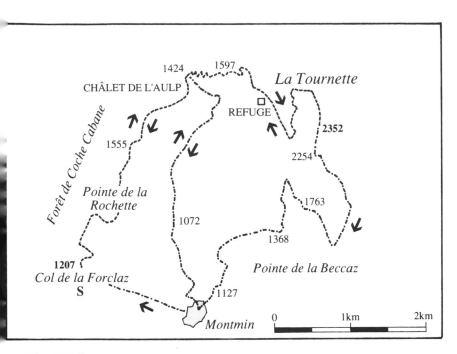

1424   1597

CHÂLET DE L'AULP

La Tournette

REFUGE

2352

Forêt de Coche Cabane

1555

2254

Pointe de la
Rochette

1763

1072

1368

1207
Col de la Forclaz
S

Pointe de la Beccaz

1127

Montmin

0   1km   2km

The Walk

From the Col de la Forclaz, take the obvious path to the north-east. This is part of the long-distance route GR96 and the Tour of Lake Annecy and leads without difficulty, but climbing steadily, to the Col de l'Aulp in 3km (2 miles). This col is the point at which the real ascent starts. Alternatively, from the parking place above Montmin follow either the stony road or a more direct track up to the col, signposted 'Chalet de l'Aulp'.

The climb from the col is initially through pastures, becoming rocky after a few hundred metres and keeping generally to the left of the mountain. The path is always clear but, like any mountain ascent, this walk should not be attempted in misty weather. A traverse to the right above a cliff leads slightly downhill to a refuge hut, where refreshments can be obtained in season. There is a large cliff in front; the path goes to the right then swings back left in a long traverse to the Col du Varo. Another twist to the right, edging through several rocky areas, and the summit is reached.

The views are breathtaking, embracing a vast panorama of mountains and valleys. Close at hand, the formidable pinnacles of the Dents de Lanfon and Lanfonnet are reduced to apparent insignificance.

The IGN map shows two alternative footpaths from the summit of La

Tournette. The intrepid walker could use either to make a circular route, in particular that which leaves the mountain to the south, over the Pointe de la Bajulaz, ending at Montmin. However, the distance is much greater and there is a section shown as hazardous; most walkers should be content with their achievement and return by the same route.

Walk 7   Annecy: Le Parmelan 1,832m (6,010ft)

Map no:	IGN 1:50,000: 2; Bornes-Bauges
Walking time:	$3^1/_2$ – 4 hours
Grading:	Moderate with some mountain walking
Ascent:	625m (2,050ft)
Highest altitude:	1,832m (6,009ft)
Lowest altitude:	1,207m (3,959ft)

As with La Tournette, this is very much a mountain ascent. There is, however, more interest and variety in the route and its immediate landscape. Le Parmelan is the mountain which, from Annecy, sits behind the lower Mont Veyrier. It is visible from a long distance from the west and south-west and is impressive when seen from across Annecy lake over the Col de Bluffy, its long precipice seeming to be an impenetrable barrier. The effort and time involved is very similar to that required for a British Lake District peak such as Coniston Old Man. The path is excellent underfoot, is well-marked, and there is no danger in clear weather.

From Annecy take the D5 road, through Annecy le Vieux towards Thorens. Shortly after Villaz village turn right into the Route Forestière du Parmelan. Keep going until the road loses its surface and park in a clearing. The lower part of this access road has delightful views, at least for passengers.

The Walk

Take the broad track rising steeply to the right, towards Parmelan, reaching a large sign 'Le Parmelan par le Châlet Chapuis' and follow the arrow. The châlet is soon reached – altitude 1,250m (4,100ft) – and, after a pause to admire the view and take any necessary refreshment, the path rising to the left is followed, clearly signposted 'Parmelan'. The pasture on the left is usually well carpeted with flowers and the entrance to the ensuing woodland has plenty of blackberries. The path zigzags up through the forest, bearing left at another signpost.

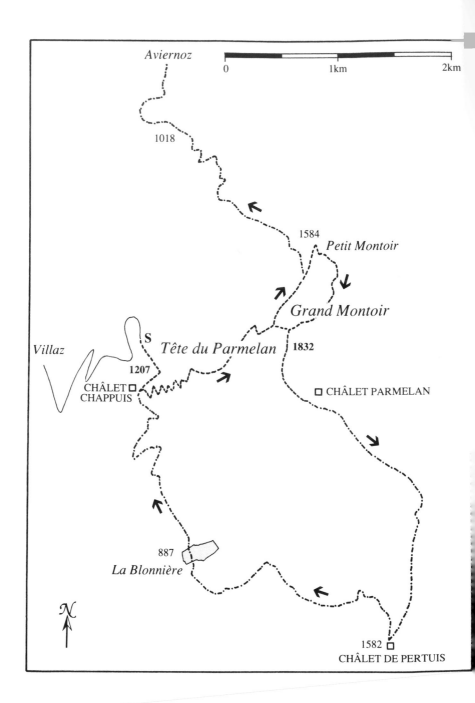

Aviernoz

0   1km   2km

1018

1584
Petit Montoir

Grand Montoir

S
Villaz   Tête du Parmelan   1832

1207

CHÂLET
CHAPPUIS

CHÂLET PARMELAN

887
La Blonnière

N

1582
CHÂLET DE PERTUIS

Under the cliff face of Le Parmelan

By this time the walker may be rather uncomfortably aware that he is very close to the foot of an enormous rock face and that his destination lies above and behind that impossible and impassable barrier. At the next sign, 'Boucle du Parmelan. Refuge Dunand', swing left and follow a most delightful path along the foot of the great cliff.

Part way across the cliff foot, the next sign is reached 'Boucle du Parmelan – Petit Montoir'. Here there may be a parting of the ways amongst the members of the walking party. More specifically, the route up to the right is the Grand Montoir, undoubtedly the shortest way to the top, utilising a fault in the cliff face. However, it is steep and difficult and cut steps and iron chains have been provided to aid the ascent. It should not be attempted by anyone without a good head for heights. Most walkers will prefer the Petit Montoir, which carries on to the left and outflanks the cliff, providing a very safe route, eventually turning right to reach a broad plateau which slants up towards the summit, now visible to the right. The way is indicated by yellow paint markings.

The plateau is most remarkable and is described as a 'rock glacier'. The tilting surface is abundantly crevassed and a surprisingly rich plant life, including small trees, softens what would otherwise be a harsh landscape. The path winds across this section, passing the top of the Grand Montoir

The Rock Glacier

route and soon reaches the refuge, with the summit (*tête*), marked by a cross with one arm missing and a stone cairn. Not unexpectedly, the summit itself is not the best part of this mountain, nevertheless, it stands proudly enough and, in fine weather, is a place to linger. The views are magnificent covering Annecy, part of the lake, La Tournette, Mont Blanc, the Aravis chain, and much more. There is also a deep depression beloved of fossil hunters.

A return by the same route is recommended, but there are other options. It must first be said that descent by the Grand Montoir is not really an option except for those very experienced in exposed scrambling. Walkers wanting a longer return route can leave the summit to the south, towards the Col de Pertuil. After negotiating a tricky section, this route turns sharp right descending to the hamlet of La Blonnière and continuing to the Châlet Chapuis and the car parking. Yet another option leaves the mountain to the north towards Aviernoz, for some distance sharing the route with the Petit Montoir path, to reach a forestry road which climbs very high to the Chalet de l'Anglette, where cars may be left. It is not possible to combine this route with Villaz to make a circuit, without road-walking between Aviernoz and Villaz, or special transport arrangements.

Walk 8 Annecy (La Clusaz): Tête du Danay 1,731m (5,679ft)

Map no:	IGN 1:50,000: 8; Mont Blanc Beaufortain
Walking time:	2 hours
Grading:	Moderate with some mountain walking
Ascent:	320m (1,050ft)
Highest altitude:	1,731m (5,678ft)
Lowest altitude:	1,411m (4,628ft)

This walk reaches the summit of a small peak in the Confins valley above La Clusaz. The summit provides the best viewpoint for the spectacular Aravis chain of mountains. The walking is straightforward and the route is well signposted. About 2 hours should be allowed for the short versions.

From Annecy, drive to Thônes, either via the Col de Bluffy (D909) or the road to the north of Mont Veyrier (D18). At Thônes bear left towards St Jean de Sixt and La Clusaz (D909). At La Clusaz, bear left again and climb the valley road to Les Confins. At the top of the hamlet, by a tiny church dedicated to two heroes of the *maquis*, is the Départ de Confins, an official starting place for walking routes. There is a sign board indicating the way to Le Danay, among others, with a suggested ascent time of 1 hour 20 minutes. Car parking should not be difficult.

The Walk

Start off down the roadway to the left and, after 100m, take a road on the right, signposted to 'Tête du Danay'. The surfaced road soon gives way to a trackway, again signposted, which rises quite steeply. The views of the Aravis are splendid and the countryside generally is much more Alpine than the Annecy lake area. At a well-signposted junction, bear left. The path is very scenic and eventually a farm is reached at a minor col, where local cheese may be purchased. Carry on up a grassy shoulder, heading for woodland, with a fringe of rowan trees ablaze with berries in late summer.

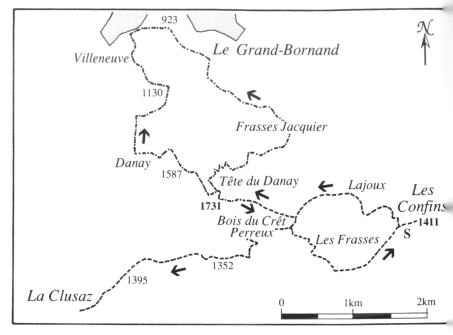

The way is now along a broad ridge, with pine trees, bilberry plants and even a little heather. A small clearing is reached, with a signpost, and the summit is just above, to the right. There is a large cross, constructed of angle iron, a board indicating 'Le Danay Alt. 1,730m', and a strategically-placed seat. Evidence of an abundant rabbit population should not be allowed to detract from this summit as one of the finest picnic spots in Haute-Savoie. Large yellow and black butterflies flutter from flower to flower and ravens swoop above the trees, but most important of all is the view. The jagged outline of the Aravis brings to mind the Cuillins of Skye, but on a grander scale. La Clusaz and its outlying hamlets are down below, with the chalets and Alpine pastures stretching well up the valley sides. Descend to the clearing with the signpost and decide on a return route. To return by the same route takes rather less than 1 hour and an alternative short way back to the starting place is to walk down to the farm at the col and then turn right down a forest track signposted 'Les Frasses' and then right again at a sign for 'La Clusaz par Les Frasses', swinging left quite shortly at yet another sign 'Les Frasses: La Clusaz'. The track descends steeply through the forest, parts of which are deeply rutted by tractor tyres and would be unpleasant after rain. On reaching the hamlet of Les Frasses, turn left on the metalled road and join the main valley road, bearing left to return to Les Confins in about 1¹/₂km (1 mile).

The chapel at Les Confins

Other options from the sign by the summit of Le Danay are clearly posted. There are two routes leading to Grand-Bornand village, one starting to the right and one to the left; La Clusaz, starting to the left, as for Les Frasses (above) and diverting to the right shortly after the farm; and St Jean de Sixt, to the right.

All these routes are well-posted and easy to follow, but a finish other than at Les Confins will necessitate assistance in moving a car, as public transport above La Clusaz, other than a winter ski bus, is non-existent.

Walk 9   Annecy (Thônes): The Roman Bridge

Map no:	IGN 1:50,000: 2; Bornes-Bauges
Walking time:	2 hours
Grading:	Easy
Ascent:	Very little
Highest altitude:	665m (2,181ft)
Lowest altitude:	625m (2,050ft)

Signposted walks are very well organised in and around Thônes and vary from strenuous ascents to mountain peaks to quite gentle rambles. This walk is very much one of the latter and can be recommended, almost without reservation, for all the family. There is no significant ascent. The time taken can be reduced if a shorter version is preferred.

Thônes is reached from Annecy either via the Col de Bluffy (D909) or the alternative road passing to the north of Mont Veyrier (D18). On entering Thônes an area of parkland is evident on the right. At the end of this area almost opposite the church is the tourist office. Turn sharp right and find car parking along the side of the minor road leading to a bridge over the river Fier.

The Walk

Cross over the river and turn left into a very minor road, the Chemin de Paradis, with a clear signpost 'Sentier du Pont Romain 26', the 26 being the local footpath numbering system. When the roadway bends right, carry on along the unsurfaced trackway ahead. The well-posted track keeps close to the river, passing through attractive woodland with blackberries in places by the wayside.

The walker is often conscious of the proximity of a road and of some industry across the river but, on the whole, the screening is good and a pleasant riverside walk can be enjoyed, with abundant plant and bird life. To the right are hilly pastures and forest, and behind is the huge cliff which forms the end of Le Grand Biollay.

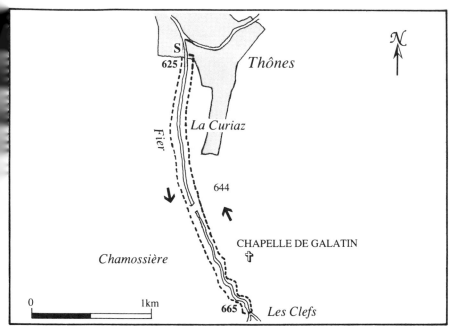

A small tributary of the river Fier is crossed on a wooden bridge and the Pont de Chamossière is reached at a metalled road. Turn right and walk up the metalled road until a sign is reached at the far side of a large house. Turn left into another metalled road and, as the road bends right, take the signposted footpath to the left. This section of the route is along a narrow path descending through woodland to return to the river bank. On reaching the next roadway, with a bridge over the river, carry straight on along the water's edge. Ascend a mini zigzag, which could be slippery after rain, and carry on to reach the Pécherat bridge. Cross this to the main Thônes – Faverges road and walk back along the road to the left for 100m. Cross over and follow the sign to the Pont Romain. This interesting bridge is in surprisingly good condition and can still be used to walk over the river.

To return to Thônes the most pleasant route is to retrace steps along the path. However, the road is not too busy and provides a quicker route to the town. A compromise is to use the road as far as the Chamossière bridge, cross over, and return from that point by the footpath.

For a shorter excursion, there is limited parking near the Chamossière bridge and a round trip from there to the Pont Romain would take about 1 hour. To reach the bridge by car, leave Thônes by the road to Serraval and Faverges (D12) and turn right in $1^1/_2$km (almost 1 mile) from the town

The end of the ridge at Thônes

centre, at a sign 'Chamossière'. The bridge is reached in a short distance. Park your car near a large map illustrating local footpaths.

Walk 10   Chamonix: Chamonix – Montenvers

Map no:	IGN 1:50,000: 8; Mont Blanc Beaufortain
Walking time:	2 hours
Grading:	Moderate with continuous downhill walking
Descent:	853m (2,798ft)
Highest altitude:	1,913m (6,276ft)
Lowest altitude:	1,060m (3,478ft)

Rather perversely, this walk starts with a train ride. However, it is no ordinary train ride, but an ascent by rack railway from Chamonix at 1,060m (3,478 ft) to Montenvers at 1,913m (6,276ft). The latter is situated at the edge of the Mer de Glace, arguably the finest of the many glaciers of the Mont Blanc *massif*. The actual walking is all downhill. Whilst this obviously demands less physical effort, the effect on the legs, particularly of those unaccustomed to mountain walking, should not be underestimated. Nearly 900m (2,952ft) is a long way down! The path is generally rough and stony but is very clear and easy to follow.

The special station for the Montenvers railway is situated behind the SNCF station in Chamonix. It is well-signposted and the main road along the valley passes very close by, over a level crossing virtually at the end of the platform. There is some car parking in front of the station building and a great deal more within 5 minutes walk. In high season, trains run at 20 minute intervals, but at other times there is a less frequent service. The journey takes 20 minutes but is not cheap. In 1989 a single adult ticket cost 34 francs (£3.40). Return tickets are, pro rata, somewhat cheaper.

The trip is, however, 20 minutes of sheer delight as the line climbs steeply among magnificent scenery. The destination is Montenvers, which comprises an hotel, the odd café/bar, a gift shop, a small museum and terraces with breathtaking views of the glacier and various parts of the Mont Blanc range, particularly the Grands Jorasses and the Aiguilles des Drus and Verte. There is also an ice cave in the side of the glacier, which may be visited by using a

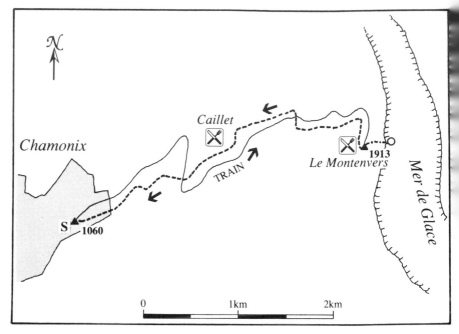

footpath or a *télé-cabine* lift down a steep hillside. Several footpaths start at Montenvers, and this walk is a straightforward descent to Chamonix.

The Walk

From the station, follow the railway back to the Montenvers hotel. Turn left at the hotel and look for a sign indicating 'Chamonix – 1 hour 45 minutes', and proceed down to the right. The route is very easy to follow, through light woodland of pine and rowan trees, with a few wild raspberries evident in season. A superb viewpoint for photographing the railway is soon reached, close to a viaduct. The track carries on largely in zigzags and the views of the Brévent and the Aiguilles Rouges on the far side of the valley are excellent.

The railway is crossed and a refreshment hut is reached at Caillet at 1,530m (5,018ft), almost half-way down. The terrace to this café is spectacular but should clearly not be overloaded with customers. Below Caillet, Chamonix itself and the outlying villages become more prominent, almost beneath your feet. You will see black butterflies with yellow-edged wings in summer, as they are disturbed by the passage of walkers.

The railway is again crossed, at a double-tracked passing loop, and the track reaches a skiing area close to an artificial toboggan run (*luge d'été*). Pass the bottom end of this run on the right, followed by Les Planards bar/ restaurant, and a large car parking area to return to the level crossing and the Montenvers – Mer de Glace station.

Walk 11   Chamonix: Le Brévent – 2,525m (8,284ft)

Map no:	IGN 1:50,000: 8; Mont Blanc Beaufortain
Walking time:	7 hours
Grading:	Experienced with a lot of mountain walking
Ascent:	1,370m (4,500ft)
Highest altitude:	2,525m (8,284ft)
Lowest altitude:	1,160m (3,805ft)

Le Brévent is a fine mountain in its own right. It is the dominant peak adjacent to Chamonix on the side of the valley opposite Mont Blanc and is greatly valued as a viewpoint. The climb from Merlet is no more difficult than that of one of the bigger British mountains, but does require 963m (3,159ft) of ascent. The full circuit set out below increases the total ascent to about 1,370m (4,500ft). Walkers with mountain experience should allow about 7 hours for the circuit.

From Chamonix it is a short drive along the main valley road to Les Houches. Leave this road at the sign 'Les Houches – Chef Lieu' and fork right towards the railway station. Before the station, turn right again into a little road which crosses the railway on a narrow bridge and then climbs steadily up the hillside. On reaching a junction, turn right heading for the animal park at Merlet. After a short distance the road loses its surface; carry on regardless until you reach a further surfaced section. Quite shortly you will reach a notice prohibiting further driving. There is space here to park.

The Walk

Carry on by walking up the broad, stony track, soon reaching the gate of the animal park, which has many specimens of local animals as a tourist attraction but is open only in high season. Strike off to the right up a prominent track with the park boundary fence on the left. The woodland on the left is usually alive with small birds, largely of the tit family, and the view across to two of the great Mont Blanc glaciers, des Bossons and de Taconnaz,

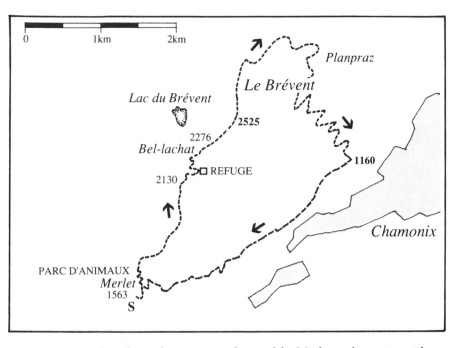

is impressive. Just above the perimeter fence of the Merlet park, a point with several signs is reached. Take a narrow track up to the right following a sign for 'Bel-lachat'. This route is part of GR5, the Tour de Mont Blanc and the Sentier du Pays de Mont Blanc, and it is marked by red and white paint stripes on rocks and trees. After a slope rich in bilberry plants, the path crosses a rocky valley; the far side involves some modest rock scrambling, assisted by a metal rail and foot rests. In one or two places there is a feeling of exposure which could worry walkers with no head for heights. Bird life is now more sparse, but Alpine choughs will probably be circling overhead. Although the landscape is now very similar to the UK, it is noticeable that there are paint marks instead of stone cairns marking the way. In $1^1/_2$ to 2 hours the Cantine de Bel-lachat at 2,152m (7,059ft) is reached. This is a typical mountain refuge/refreshment hut open only in season.

The track carries on, bending sharply to the left just before the hut and rising. A stone construction advising of the 'Reserve Naturelle des Aiguilles Rouges' is reached next, with several direction signs. Bear right towards Le Brévent and the Lac de Brévent, passing another Brévent sign. A completely new view now opens up to the left – a chain of mountains, the Rochers des Fiz, ending in a great buttress on the right flank.

The peak of the Brévent is now in sight. Alas, it is not entirely a pretty sight, with the meccano-like structure of the cabin lift terminus horribly prominent. Lake Brévent is also now in view and can be reached by a minor path branching off through the jumbled rocks to the left. Very quiet and observant walkers may well see marmots dashing from rock to rock in this area. The level section of path ends and the stony waste of the summit must now be climbed. The path is not always entirely clear, but the red and white paint signs are a great help. At a sign pointing the way back, turn sharp right to reach the summit.

Despite the man-made accretions, including a snack-bar, this is a marvellous place, with a rather dilapidated orientation table helping to identify the scores of peaks all around. The feeling of near parity in height with all except the Mont Blanc group is particularly gratifying. Out of season, when the cabin lift has closed, the peak may well be deserted and consequently be a much more select place. In the generally extensive view, Mont Blanc is outstanding. Whatever doubts there may have been from the valley below concerning the actual summit, there is no doubt from here; the noble white dome stands head and shoulders above the more spectacular rocky pinnacles which guard it on all sides.

The return to Merlet can be by the same route, taking about 2 hours, or by completing a longer circuit. If the latter is desired, descend from the summit and turn right, making for the Col du Brévent and Planpraz along a wide trackway. A choice between the Tour de Mont Blanc pathway and the ski piste is soon offered, the ski piste being more direct. Bear right and aim for the ski-lift station clearly in view below. From here, there are no less than four routes down to the Petit Balcon Sud, which is the next objective. A high level route, via Plan Lachat, has one slightly difficult section and is less direct. The most obvious is to use the unsurfaced roadway, initially via Planpraz (the cabin lift station) which zigzags interminably down towards Chamonix. There are paths, following much the same line, both to east and west of this roadway, which are undoubtedly more interesting. The main compensation for the rather monotonous roadway descent is that the good walking surface permits full enjoyment of the views. When Chamonix is very near indeed look out for a path at the end of a right-hand zig (or zag?). This is signposted as the 'Petit Balcon Sud'. Turn right for the return to Merlet. This is a terraced trackway contouring beautifully through woodland, which is more fully described in Walk 16. For this walk, keep to Petit Balcon Sud at every intersection. After crossing a dry stream bed, branch up to the right at a signpost 'Merlet − 1 hour 10 minutes'. At the next junction, again fork right, uphill, still following 'Merlet'. A set of wooden steps completes this rather

Mont Blanc from Merlet

arduous ascent, to join the unsurfaced road a little way above the parking area. Turn left downhill, following the sign 'Les Bossons: Chamonix' to return to the starting point.

Walk 12 Chamonix: Argentière – Petits Balcons

Map no:	IGN 1:50,000: 8; Mont Blanc Beaufortain
Walking time:	3 hours
Grading:	Moderate with one short hard ascent
Ascent:	Moderate
Highest altitude:	1,305m (4,280ft)
Lowest altitude:	1,185m (3,887ft)

The Petit Balcon Sud and Petit Balcon Nord are generally excellent footpaths running along each side of the Chamonix valley for several kilometres. Subject to the geography, they endeavour to maintain a constant, modest height above the valley floor. At frequent intervals, paths rise to meet the *Balcons*, facilitating circular walks of variable duration. This circuit from Argentière uses both *Balcons* and requires about 3 hours' walking time. It may be shortened by returning by train from the station at Lajoux. The only steep ascent is from the valley to join the Petit Balcon Nord, a hard, short pull of about 120m (400ft). Incidentally, note that, with perfect Gallic logic, the Petit Balcon Sud is on the north side of the valley and vice versa.

There is ample car parking space at the railway station in Argentière at the lower end of the main street. Alternatively, there is a reasonable local train service from Chamonix and other stations all along the valley.

The Walk

From the car park turn left at the main street and then right into a prominent trackway, immediately before reaching the railway line. Follow the signpost 'Petit Balcon Sud'. After a tree endowed with many notices, the track gains height above the railway line and continues as an easily followed path, good underfoot, and with some blackberry bushes. A more open section crosses a slope of large scree and you reach an attractive wooden bridge over a small tributary of the river Arve. At a junction, carry straight on. The path to the left is signposted to 'Le Grassonet', whilst that to the right leads to a training

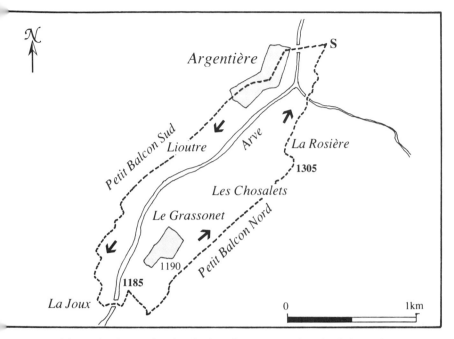

ground for a climbing school. The low-lying ground to the left is a favourite area for coal tits. At an intersection, leave the Petit Balcon Sud, following a sign to the left 'Jonction avec Petit Balcon Nord. Lajoux' and descend to a wide grassy track across a field and the hamlet of Lajoux. Turn sharp left following another sign for the 'Jonction' and cross the railway at Lajoux station.

Turn right down the unsurfaced roadway and, in 100m, turn left at a white house. There is yet another of the 'Jonction' signs to confirm the route which has the distinction of being the Chemin des Cordays. Just before the river there is a signpost; here you follow the track for Argentière, and very shortly, at another intersection, bear right at a familiar Jonction sign. Cross over the river Arve on a wooden bridge, turn left along the main road for 50m, and then right into a pathway signposted 'Jonction avec Petit Balcon Nord'.

After crossing a field, enter woodland and climb steeply to join the Petit Balcon Nord. Turn left at the signpost 'Argentière'. The forest is mainly pine, with some deciduous areas, and sufficient gaps to enjoy the views across the valley. Part of this track was artificially constructed in 1973 and the result is a fine rambling route, descending gently and easy underfoot. At an intersection carry straight on for Argentière, noting the height of 1,247m (4,115ft). After a short uphill section, look for a posting 'Petit Balcon' and fork left. At the next junction, keep left, still following 'Argentière'.

Jacques Balmat shows De Saussure the route to the top of Mont Blanc, Chamonix

At a large clearing – La Rosière – go straight across towards Argentière and reach a large concrete tunnel, richly decorated with graffiti. Cross the unsurfaced road and carry on past a rock with a yellow arrow. The signpost is now for 'Le Tour'. The river is crossed on a plank bridge, bearing left; at a T-junction by a chalet turn left, following a sign for 'Argentière', and pass under the railway to reach a surfaced road. Go straight ahead towards the centre of the village, passing its prettiest area with the odd decorated chalet and the church, noted for its baroque internal decoration. At the main road, turn left downhill to return to the station.

Walk 13   Chamonix: Grand Balcon Nord

Map no:	IGN 1:50,000: 8; Mont Blanc Beaufortain
Walking time:	6$^1/_2$ hours
Grading:	Moderate
Ascent:	1,220m (4,000ft)
Highest altitude:	2,233m (7,324ft)
Lowest altitude:	1,060m (3,478ft)

The Grand Balcon Nord is a high level footpath terracing along the northern flank of the Mont Blanc range of mountains, most of the path being at an altitude of greater than 1,830m (6,000ft). The section between Montenvers and the Plan de l'Aiguille is a deservedly popular walk, and several possible variations may be used, depending upon the time and energy available. The shorter versions will be mentioned at the appropriate place in the text.

There is a fair amount of free car parking by the SNCF railway station in Chamonix. Alternatively, across the main road, towards the Planards restaurant, is an enormous cleared area available for car parking.

The Walk

The walk starts by the railway level crossing, making for the Planards restaurant and continuing uphill close by the summer toboggan run (*luge d'été*). Carry on up an obvious ski run, looking carefully for a track which goes off to the left part way up the ski slope. Once found, this track to Montenvers rises steadily at a fairly even gradient, largely in zigzags, and with a fair amount of woodland in the upper reaches. It is extremely easy to follow and with a generally good walking surface. It is never far from the railway line, which is crossed twice and there are opportunities for striking photographs of the little red trains. The refreshment hut of Caillet, at roughly the half-way stage to Montenvers is open in high season. Views across the valley are splendid almost all the way to the top, which should be reached after 2$^1/_2$ hours of hard climbing.

The first and most obvious economy of time and effort is to use the railway from Chamonix to Montenvers. Twenty minutes of pleasant riding replace $2^1/_2$ hours of uphill toil but, of course, at a cost. A single adult fare in 1989 was 34 francs (£3.50) a return was 46 francs (£4.75).

Having reached Montenvers by whatever method, there is another immediate choice. The Grand Balcon Nord has two alternative routes for the first section of about $1^1/_2$km (1 mile). From the Montenvers hotel, the left-hand route, signposted at the 'Musée – temple de la nature' to 'Plan de l'Aiguille' is by the Signal, a minor peak, with a suggested walking time of 2 hours 40 minutes. This is quite straightforward, but does involve about 125m (410 ft) of extra ascent. The other route, signposted to the same destination, is slightly more direct, with a suggested time of 2 hours 15 minutes. It does, however, have some exposed sections which are not advised for those with no head for heights. This route needs care in starting from the hotel. It is easy to bear too far left, where there are inviting-looking stone steps leading to a jumble of rocks. Disregard these and proceed quite close to the back of a row of hotel outbuildings, rising gently as the buildings are left behind. As a ruin is passed on the left look for a marking of red paint on a rock. The exposed section is reached as a small valley is crossed, with a man-made wall assisting the walker across the head of the valley. Chamonix is clearly visible almost 1,000 metres below, as a small building is passed on the right. The path clings to the mountainside and frequent stops are necessary to do justice to the views, in which Le Brévent is particularly prominent. The path via Le Signal joins on the left, at a sign describing the two routes to Montenvers; 'vue panoramique' for the high route, and 'raccourci escarpé' (steep short cut) for the lower route.

At this point, a perfectly valid option is to return to Montenvers by the route other than that used for the outward journey, making an excellent circular walk of about 4km ($2^1/_2$ miles) from Montenvers and possibly taking advantage of the better-value return fare on the railway.

However, the Grand Balcon carries on to the Plan de l'Aiguille as a superb path, now free from exposed sections and rising gently across open upland, with the rocky spire of the Aiguille du Midi ahead, set against the white bulk of Mont Blanc itself. The next option for a short route is to turn right at a sign for 'Chamonix par Blaitière'. This track down is well-defined and proceeds through some most attractive broken country, past the ruins of Blaitière dessus (upper) and Blaitière dessous (lower), aiming obviously straight for Chamonix.

Below Blaitière dessous, the path swings left, to reach a junction with a broken sign. The most direct route to the parking area is down to the right,

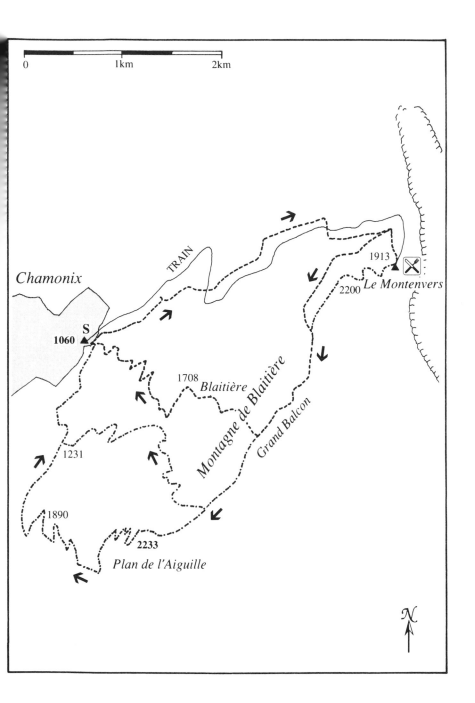

Chamonix

TRAIN

1060 S

1708 Blaitière

Montagne de Blaitière

Grand Balcon

1231

1890

2233

Plan de l'Aiguille

1913

2200 Le Montenvers

N

The Aiguille du Midi from the Grand Balcon Nord

although to carry straight on, with a later right turn, will also lead to Chamonix. The track to the right descends steeply through thick woodland, zigzagging steadily. There are many steep short cuts across the zigzags which should be avoided, particularly if the ground is wet.

Quite close to Chamonix a T-junction is reached. Either route may now be chosen leading back to the large open area close to the Planards restaurant. Those who do not take the Blaitières descent will carry on to the Plan de l'Aiguille, where there is a refuge at 2,233m (7,324ft). This is close to the intermediate station on the Aiguille du Midi cabin lift – less than 1km ($^1/_2$ mile) uphill to the left – and an obvious easy way down is to use this lift.

Those descending on foot have two options, right or left, for the long descent to Chamonix. Distances are roughly similar, on well-defined paths ending on a minor road, leading to the main road less than 1km ($^1/_2$ mile) west of the car park. However, the right-hand path has a connection with the lower portion of the Blaitières route, about half-way down, which can be used to return directly to the car park.

Walk 14 Chamonix: Le Prarion 1,967m (6,453ft)

Map no:	IGN 1:50,000: 8; Mont Blanc Beaufortain
Walking time:	4 – 5$^1/_2$ hours
Grading:	Moderate
Ascent: (on foot)	314m (1,030ft)
Highest altitude:	1,967m (6,453ft)
Lowest altitude:	993m (3,257ft)

Le Prarion is a comparatively minor mountain but, like so many such mountains, is a superb viewpoint. The cabin lift from Les Houches to Bellevue gives a flying start to this walk, which is entirely on good paths. The section from Bellevue to the Prarion hotel is almost like walking along a country lane at an altitude of 1,700m (nearly 5,600ft) with unexpectedly abundant vegetation. The savage rocks and glaciers of Mont Blanc are behind and the immediate surroundings are entirely gentle. This is, in fact, prime ski country and lifts of all types abound. There are several options for a longer or shorter walk but the full round requires about 4 hours, using the Bellevue cabin lift. Walking the first section will add approximately 1$^1/_2$ hours to this time.

Les Houches village is easily reached from Chamonix by car, bus or train. The starting point is the bottom of the Bellevue cabin lift by the roadside, just a little way west of the church and village centre. There is a good car parking area beside the cabin-lift building.

The Walk

In just 5 minutes by cabin, Bellevue is reached at 1,794m (5,884ft). (1989 fares – 29 francs (£3) single, 46 francs (£4.75) return.) Outside the station is a prominent notice board, pointing the way to the Col de Voza and the Mont Blanc tramway. It may, in fact, come as a surprise to find a rudimentary station close by, a calling place for trains on the railway which runs for several kilometres from Le Fayat/St Gervais to the side of a glacier at high altitude

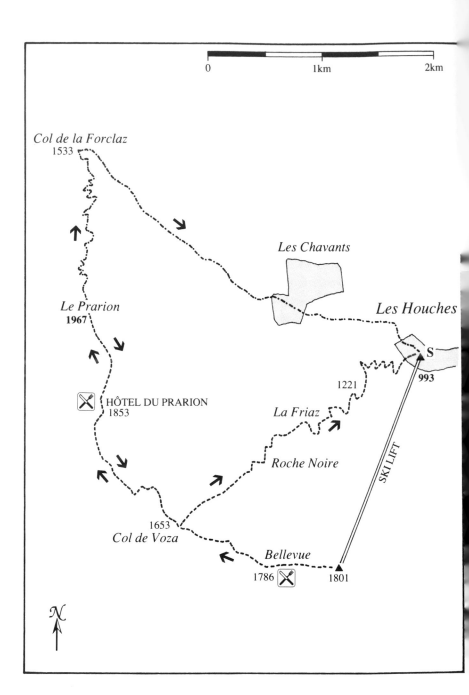

Col de la Forclaz
1533

Les Chavants

Le Prarion
1967

Les Houches

S

993

1221

HÔTEL DU PRARION
1853

La Friaz

Roche Noire

SKI LIFT

1653
Col de Voza

Bellevue

1786

1801

N

– Le Nid d'Aigle. In season, refreshments are obtainable at Bellevue.

From the notice board head towards the Col de Voza, descending slightly, with the railway on the left. The track, a variant of the Tour de Mont Blanc, is broad and the surroundings quite surprisingly pastoral for the altitude. Pass the Hotel Bellevue and cross the railway, following signs for 'Col de Voza' and 'Les Houches'.

The col – 1,658m (5,438ft) – is soon reached, with its quite sumptuous hotel and a small railway depot. There are many signs and it will be noted that GR5 and the Tour de Mont Blanc path both cross this col. Carry on along the broad trackway rising straight ahead, signed by a blue and yellow fingerpost, heading for 'Le Delevret' and 'St Gervais par Le Prarion'. The track forks immediately, so take the left-hand, higher route making for yet another hotel visible on the skyline. The view behind, which combines the gleaming white dome of Mont Blanc with a foreground of gentle mixed woodland, is an amazing contrast. Keep straight on at a junction, heading for Le Prarion hotel-restaurant – 1,860m (6,101ft).

Pass closely behind the hotel, and then close to the cabin-lift building, following signs to 'Col de la Forclaz', not to be confused with the col of the same name close to Annecy lake. The summit of the Prarion is clearly in view ahead, and a wooden sign close to the cabin-lift indicates a path bearing right and upwards for 'Tête du Prarion' and 'Col de la Forclaz', marked with a large red arrow.

The nature of the walk has suddenly become quite different; it is now a small path meandering among rocks and light woodland, with the occasional small pool. Despite the steady ascent it is entirely delightful and perfectly safe for all. There are two variants of this path, and either may be taken with confidence. Red marks on the rocks confirm the way to the summit.

The description *vue unique*, used on the sign near the hotel, is more than justified. In all directions it is superb and on some days there is cloud below, with the mountain peaks floating above like dark icebergs. There is a wonderful feeling of elevation yet with total safety. This is certainly a place to linger.

For the return there are several options. The most ambitious is to carry on along the ridge of Le Prarion and to drop to the Col de la Forclaz. From the col a path back to Les Houches bears to the right and descends to Les Granges des Chavants, Les Chavants hamlet and then Les Houches. However, a short section of the end of Le Prarion ridge is very steep, the path is narrow and is recommended only for those who are sure-footed and clear-headed in exposed places. It is generally earth underfoot, and could be slippery in wet weather. You have been warned! If in doubt, it is only 5 minutes' walk from the summit of Le Prarion to reach this section and to make your own decision.

Having taken full advantage of the views from the summit, there is no shame in retracing steps to the Col de Voza, as such a delightful path is worth a second passage.

From the Col de Voza, there are two paths down to Les Houches. The slightly more direct path is part of GR5 and the Tour de Mont Blanc. It passes close to the hotel, to the right, crossing an area of soft ground, and descends past the bottom end of a ski-lift. There are surprisingly muddy sections of this track but it is very well-defined after the first 100m or so. A sign 'Col de Voza – 30 minutes' is passed and the track carries on down to the right. On a straight section there is a long view of the colossal statue of Christ the King on the far side of the valley. This is illuminated after dark. Pass an old chalet 'La Friaz Alt. 1,329 metres' with a small sign pointing upwards to three destinations.

The Chamonix valley is now fully revealed, with the enormous gravel workings near Les Houches being unfortunately prominent. The hamlet of Belleface is reached and care must be taken to leave the metalled road as it bends left for a track on the right, signposted 'Les Houches'. This track reaches the village very close to the cabin-lift station and car parking. Total walking time from Bellevue to Les Houches is about $3^1/_2$ hours.

Those walkers wanting an even shorter route and not caring for long descents may well book return tickets on the cabin-lift and return to Bellevue from the Col de Voza.

Walk 15   Chamonix: Les Houches – River Arve

Map no:	IGN 1:50,000: 8; Mont Blanc Beaufortain
Walking time:	1 – 1½ hours
Grading:	Easy
Ascent:	Negligible
Highest altitude:	1,020m (3,345ft)
Lowest altitude:	1,000m (3,280ft)

Because of the geography, most walks in the Chamonix valley will involve significant ascents and descents. This is only to be expected: after all, Mont Blanc, king of European mountains, forms one side of the valley, whilst the slopes leading to the Brévent and the Aiguilles Rouges on the other side are hardly less steep.

However, not all walkers enjoy hard pounding up or down hills. This walk will suit those who enjoy rambling at its best, with well-defined tracks, no chance of losing the way, good ground underfoot, and generally pleasing views. There is also an attractive destination. However, shorter versions are possible.

The scattered village of Les Houches is situated about 9km (6 miles) west of Chamonix. From the main road, take the turning for 'Les Houches Chef Lieu' and make for the station, visible to the left. Cars may be parked in front of the station.

The Walk

Walk up the minor road to the bridge over the railway and turn right into a metalled road, signposted 'Christ Roi'. When the road loses its surface, a good track continues; bear right at a sign 'Chamonix'. A path diverges on the left, climbing steeply to the great statue of Christ Roi (Christ the King). This is an optional extra to the walk, but the ascent is quite considerable and it is not possible to obtain a good view of the statue from the actual site.

Whilst this is basically a level path, there is one mound to be surmounted,

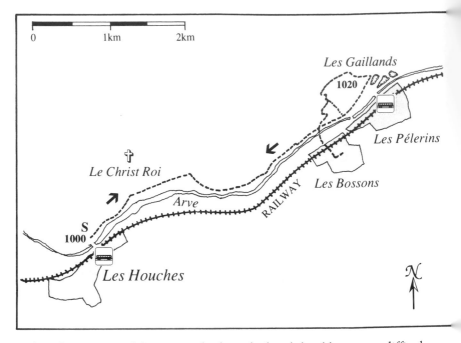

but the ascent and descent are both gradual and should cause no difficulty. At Les Houches there is a very large industrial site, apparently gravel workings. This is occasionally in view from the path, but the tree screening is good and the general environment, with abundant plant and animal life, is more than sufficient to compensate, butterflies and lizards being particularly noticeable.

As the track narrows, it becomes carpeted with pine needles, and descends almost to the level of the river Arve. A path on the left climbs up to the animal park at Merlet and the views of two of Mont Blanc's most important glaciers, des Bossons and de Taconnaz, are very fine. A footbridge on the right crosses the river, leading to Les Bossons; bear left and carry on towards Chamonix. A second bridge is soon reached, with car parking, and a picnic area in a clearing. Carry on, passing another path on the left to Merlet and Le Brévent, and then a right turn which joins the main road under a railway bridge. Ignore these and keep to the path bearing a little to the left to reach the final section, Promenade à l'Anglais, behind some houses.

This pleasant track is part of a *parcours sportif* on which those walkers still with energy to spare can test the strength and endurance of various muscles. At the end of the *parcours* is the smaller of the Gaillands lakes beautifully set among trees by a great cliff which is popular with rock climbers. This is a well-

The lake at Les Gaillands

used picnic and general recreation area which is likely to be busy in season, particularly at weekends. The Pélérins station is across the road, back a little way at the end of the larger lake.

If the train is due and time is short, cut across the road by the houses instead of entering the Promenade à l'Anglais and make straight for the station. The return journey to Les Houches takes about 10 minutes.

A shorter walk is possible by turning right at the second bridge to reach the main road, and then turning left to Les Bossons station.

Walk 16 Chamonix: Chamonix – Petit Balcon Sud

Map no:	IGN 1:50,000: 8; Mont Blanc Beaufortain
Walking time:	$1^1/_2$ hours
Grading:	Easy
Ascent:	170m (558ft)
Highest altitude:	1,230m (4,035ft)
Lowest altitude:	1,060m (3,477ft)

This walk uses another section of the Petit Balcon Sud, described in general terms in the introduction to Walk 12. It enables a start to be made virtually from the centre of Chamonix with a return by the railway which is such a useful link along the valley or, alternatively, the local bus service. There is a climb of about 170m (558ft) up to the Balcon, then a generally level walk, followed by a descent, quite steep in places.

The paths are good and should not be difficult to follow.

Cars, if used, may be parked in an area behind the church, which is very central in Chamonix.

The Walk

From the church set off up the road with the mountain rescue centre and Gendarmerie on the left. At the top of the road is the base of the Brévent cabin-lift. Turn left and, almost immediately, right into the Chemin de la Pierre à Ruskin. Carry on up this surfaced road following signs for 'Petit Balcon Sud'. The road becomes unsurfaced and a sign is reached offering alternative routes. Take the track to the left signposted 'Planpraz Brévent Sentier en Lacets'. After climbing quite steeply for a short distance, turn left into a footpath signposted 'Petit Balcon Sud', and follow a beautiful rambling track through the woodland. Cross a small stream and footpaths to left and right. Bear slightly right and uphill, always following 'Petit Balcon Sud' signs.

When an intersection is reached with a sign 'Les Bossons' turn left and zigzag downhill to cross the riverside path (*see* Walk 15), a bridge over the

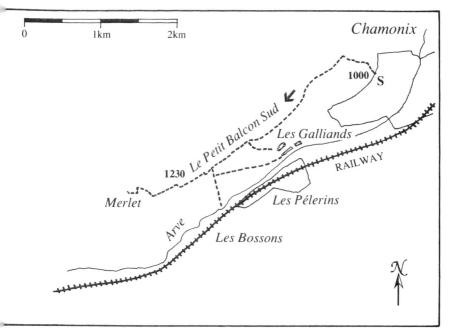

river Arve, under the railway, and turn left to reach the station for a return to Chamonix. The hillside traversed by the Petit Balcon Sud is richly vegetated and has several types of butterfly; quiet walkers may also see lizards and the occasional snake.

For a shorter version, take the path on the left leaving the Petit Balcon Sud, heading for Les Pélérins. This path drops to the attractive lakes at Les Gaillands. The railway station is close by, across the main road. Yet a third variation is to leave the Petit Balcon Sud for Les Bossons and to fork left at a signpost for Les Gaillands part way down. The riverside path can, of course, be used between Les Bossons and Les Gaillands, if desired.

Walk 17 Chamonix: Chamonix – Grand Balcon Sud

Map no:	IGN 1:50,000: 8; Mont Blanc Beaufortain
Walking time:	4 – 4$^1/_2$ hours
Grading:	Moderate to experienced
Ascent:	880m (2,886ft)
Highest altitude:	2,130m (6,986ft)
Lowest altitude:	1,250m (4,100ft)

Part of the high-level footpath known as the Grand Balcon Sud runs below the impressively craggy face of the Aiguilles Rouges. The intention is that the various Balcons will maintain more or less the same height along the valley sides for some considerable distance. The section used in this walk does achieve this for almost 3km (2 miles). However, Grands Balcons, by their very nature, are high, 2,130m (almost 7,000ft) in this instance, and the ascent from Argentière is 880m (2,886ft). For those who can enjoy a prolonged climb, this route is excellent, as it has a good path, good views and a gradient which is not excessive. The descent to the Col des Montets is generally steeper, but will not trouble walkers who enjoy mountains.

From Chamonix drive or take the train or the local bus to Argentière. Car parking is available at the station or further up the main street, turning right at the *Office de Tourisme*.

The Walk

The path starts on the opposite side of the main street, just below the Hotel de la Couronne, crosses a little stream on a plank bridge and rises steadily, passing across the back of a small building. Paint stripes of various colours will be noted, together with notices concerning the nature reserve which includes this area. A bend with a seat is reached and a more open section, with glorious views, follows, then a junction, comprehensively signposted. A right turn here will give a comparatively short, easy walk across to the road below the Col des Montets, then turning right to return to Argentière. Turn left for the

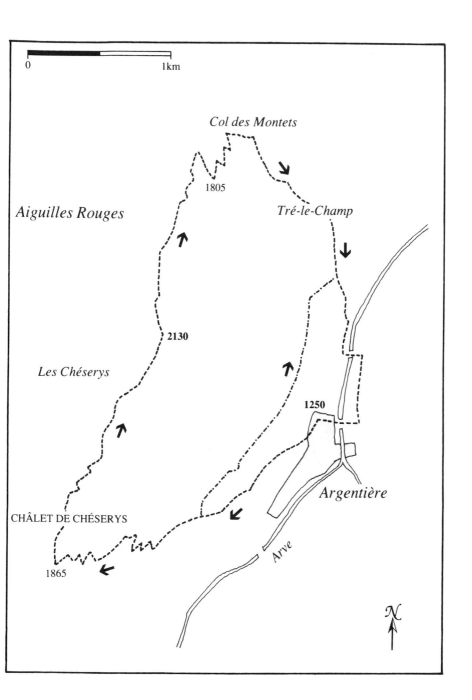

Col des Montets

1805

Aiguilles Rouges

Tré-le-Champ

2130

Les Chéserys

1250

Argentière

CHÂLET DE CHÉSERYS

1865

Arve

N

The Aiguilles Rouges from the Grand Balcon Sud

full walk, the destination being Les Chéserys. Pass two seats and reach another junction with a signpost 'Le Lac Blanc par Les Chéserys', which is followed up to the right. The barrier of the cliff face is circumvented by the skilfully routed path and a hut and large stone wall are passed. The peak of the Brévent appears in view ahead, followed by the formidable precipices of the Aiguilles Rouges, now appearing to have a genuinely rosy coloration. Apart from the occasional small bird, shyly flitting away amongst the rocks, the only life appears to be the abundant grasshoppers. Across the valley the glaciers of Argentière and Tour set off the sharply pointed peaks to perfection, whilst closer at hand a waterfall can be seen and heard across a grassy basin. The Châlet des Chéserys at 1,998m (6,553ft), is soon reached, and this is generously endowed with signs. The route lies to the right, 'Col des Montets par la Remuaz', and climbs further to reach another junction at a stone cairn. This is now the Grand Balcon Nord. Keep right, pass another stone wall and head for a large cairn on the skyline, soon reaching a nature reserve stone construction; follow the sign 'Col des Montets par la Remuaz'. The path now levels out and provides fine views of the Aiguilles Rouges as it heads towards the col. Most unusually for Savoie, the route is now marked by stone cairns.

At the next signpost bear right and begin the real descent to the col. Red arrows help to point the way across an area of jumbled rock and careful footwork is called for over much of the way down. The col is clearly in sight for most of the way. On reaching a junction with another path quite near to the road, turn right. Along this path are numerous small posts, naming a great variety of plants and trees. This is part of the nature reserve based on the Aiguilles Rouges and the building to the left, at the crest of the col, is a chalet cum laboratory, open to visitors and serving refreshments in high season. There are two 'ecological footpaths'.

The return to Argentière starts down the road to the right and can, indeed, continue by road. There is, however, a better alternative. Fork left into the minor road for Trélechamp. Pass through this hamlet and, at the point where the minor road bends up to the right to rejoin the main road, take a path on the left descending towards the main road at a lower level. After rejoining the main road for a short distance, turn left again, crossing the river at an 'Argentière' sign, and turn right into the Chemin de Vieux Four which is a pleasant walk, entering Argentière near the church.

Walk 18   Chamonix: Chamonix – Les Bois

Map no:	IGN 1:50,000: 8; Mont Blanc Beaufortain
Walking time:	2 hours
Grading:	Easy
Ascent:	Very little
Highest altitude:	1,110m (3,641ft)
Lowest altitude:	1,060m (3,477ft)

This walk is another example of a walk on level ground in mountainous country. Inevitably it has to stay fairly close to the river, following the valley bottom. The ascent is negligible, even less than in Walk 15, and there is also the advantage of starting and finishing close to the centre of Chamonix.

If a car is used, a good parking place is the area used for tennis club parking, on the right just off the Chamonix to Argentière road via Les Praz, a little way past the hospital.

The Walk

On foot from the centre of Chamonix, take the Promenade du Fori between the river Arve and the large sports complex. From the car park mentioned above, cross the river on a footbridge by the tennis courts and turn left on to the Promenade. Just after passing the last tennis court, swing right, then left and follow the Promenade des Crémeries along the side of an industrial site.

Keep straight on at the junction with Chemin des Gourgnes and follow a very straight track among the pines, reaching the Crémerie du Bois and Gîte la Montagne, where refreshments may be obtained. Keep left at a junction and, as the track angles towards a main road, swing left, then right, to cross the road and then the railway, under a pedestrian tunnel. The track is now along the Chemin d'Orthaz and a tree is reached with several signs: 'Pierre d'Orthaz; Des Bois; Sources d'Arveyron; Fontaine de Caillet; Montenvers'.

Keep to the widest and obviously main track, noting a large boulder on the right, the Pierre d'Orthaz, and carry on to reach a metalled road and a

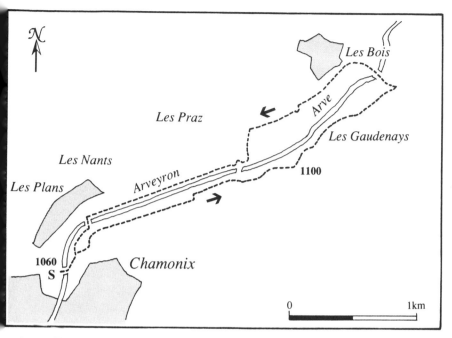

basically underground hydro-electric station, using the power of water coming down from the large glacier, the Mer de Glace, above. The road is called the Chemin des Carrières. Ignore the bridge on the left and carry on into the track opposite, with three signs, the 'Village des Bois' being the one to follow. A footpath rises to the right towards Montenvers and, in 100m, turn left over a wooden plank bridge, with signposts 'Le Lavancher; Petit Balcon Nord; Sources d'Arveyron; Le Chapeau'. At a stony clearing turn left and cross the river Arveyron by a broad wooden bridge known as the Pont Himalaya, and carry on along a wide woodland track bearing gradually left. Keep left at a sign 'Les Bois; Les Praz; Chamonix'. Shortly after, turn right then left on a metalled road; the hamlet of Les Bois is now on the right and its café/bar can be visited by making a short detour.

The return to Chamonix is first along the Route des Gaudenays, by a sign reading 'Les Praz 15 minutes'. At a bend in the road look for a windsock at the mountain rescue heliport and turn left, then immediately right, into the Chemin de la Bagna. Just before reaching the railway line turn left into the Chemin des Lots, leading to the Promenade des Bourses, where a right turn is made under the railway. Cross the road and continue close by the side of the river Arveyron. As this track ends, turn left over a wooden bridge and bear right to return along the side of the sports complex.

Walk 19 Chamonix: Les Houches – Pierre Blanche (White Stone)

Map no:	IGN 1:50,000: 8; Mont Blanc Beaufortain
Walking time:	3 – 3½ hours
Grading:	Moderate
Ascent:	670m (2,198ft)
Highest altitude:	2,000m (6,560ft)
Lowest altitude:	1,330m (4,362ft)

This is a fine mountain walk with the option of adding a worthwhile peak, the Aiguillette des Houches, to the basic circuit. Inevitably there is a considerable ascent but the path is excellent, much of the gradient easy, and the views marvellous. The forest of the lower portions is light and permits frequent views, whilst the upper section is across open mountainside. It will take an extra hour if the peak is ascended.

By car from Chamonix, take the 'Les Houches – Chef Lieu' exit from the main valley road. Turn right near Les Houches station and cross over the railway. Keep going uphill, ignoring right turns, aiming for La Flatière, until the sign for Le Bettey is reached. A wide area here provides good parking; there is no suitable space further up the road.

The Walk

Walk up the road to La Flatière, passing several large chalets as the road climbs to reach the Centre of Spiritual Retreat, where the road bends sharply to the right, soon losing its surface. The various footpath signs include 'Pierre Blanche', which is the first objective, and another notice a little further on concerns the reserve for large animals. Keep left at the next junction following the signpost 'Montvauthier. Pierre Blanche'. As a small chalet is passed, the path levels out and then turns very sharply right at another small chalet. Follow a sign 'Chailloux. Pierre Blanche', and turn left at the next junction following 'Chailloux L'Aiguillette par Pierre Blanche'. This section

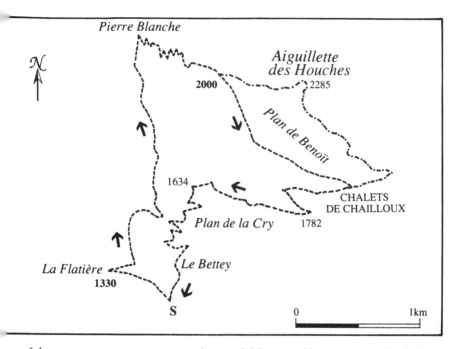

Pierre Blanche

Aiguillette
des Houches

2000   2285

Plan de Benoît

1634

CHALETS
DE CHAILLOUX

Plan de la Cry   1782

La Flatière   Le Bettey
1330

S

0   1km

of the route is most attractive with varied foliage and long views to the left opening up, with the village of Plateau d'Assy and, in the distance, the Aravis chain of mountains prominent. As the track emerges from the forest it becomes narrower and Pierre Blanche is reached. There is, alas, no great stone; in fact the only stone to be seen is a very modest affair, just right for sitting on to enjoy the view which, presumably, gives this place its particular significance. In addition to the Aravis mountains, at closer quarters are the Rochers du Fiz and, across the Gorge du Diosaz, steeply below, is the Pointe Noire de Pormena. Away to the right are the Aiguilles Rouges, whilst across the main Chamonix valley is the Col de Voza, the Prarion, the Col de la Forclaz and the Tête Noire.

From Pierre Blanche take the narrow track rising up the shoulder of the Aiguillette des Houches, signposted 'Chailloux. L'Aiguillette. Brévent'. The climb is quite steep up the broad ridge, but is entirely safe and is marked by red painted stripes on a white ground. Quite suddenly Mont Blanc appears in view ahead followed by the Aiguille du Midi, whilst, much closer, the Aiguillette des Houches is now clearly visible. The path reaches completely open mountainside – the Plan de Benoit – and achieves its summit on the 2,000m (6,560ft) contour.

This is the point of decision; the main track falls slightly as it crosses the

The Aiguilles Rouges from Pierre Blanche

Plan, a faint path to the left carries on the ascent of the shoulder leading to the peak of the Aiguillette (2,285m, 7,497ft) without serious difficulty. From the peak the most common ascent route is used for descent to the Chalets de Chailloux.

The track across the Plan de Benoit is effectively a balcon but is not so designated. It is narrow but entirely delightful, providing a good reward for the uphill toil. All too soon the Chalets de Chailloux, now in ruins, are reached.

Turn right on to a broader track and descend steadily, ignoring smaller tracks to right and left. There are no signs on this section, but white paint marks can occasionally be seen on trees. At a sharp bend look out for a patch of wild raspberries. Eventually a small clearing, the Plan de la Cry, is reached; fork right here towards La Flatière. A short cut is provided by a tiny track on the left at a sign 'Le Bettey. Les Houches'. Take this and turn left again along the side of an old broken wall, straight across at a junction with another similar sign, and reach a rough gravelled road. Turn right to return to the metalled road, then left downhill to the parking area.

Walk 20 Morzine/Samoëns/Taninges: Lac de Roy and Lac de Montriond

Map no:	(a) & (b) IGN 1:50,000: 3; Chablais, Faucigny, Genevois
Walking time:	(a) & (b) 1 hour
Grading:	(a) & (b) Easy
Ascent:	(a) 160m (525 ft) (b) there is no significant ascent
Highest altitude:	(a) 1,661m (5,448ft) (b) 1,069m (3,506ft)
Lowest altitude:	(a) 1,501m (4,923ft) (b) 1,060m (3,477ft)

Two short walks, not particularly close together and not intended to be done in sequence, but having a common theme in the circuit of a lake. There the similarity really ends.

The Lac de Roy is a lake of modest size in an attractive mountain setting. The short walk does include about 160m (525ft) of ascent, but the gradient is gentle and the actual circuit of the lake is a pleasant ramble.

The Lac de Montriond is a larger lake, set beside a minor road, with woods and cliffs providing an attractive background. The surroundings are altogether more civilised, with several hotels, restaurants and tea rooms. There is no significant ascent, the route is always obvious and the path is wide and easy.

For the **Lac de Roy walk**, turn from the road between Morzine and Taninges (D902) on to the road signposted 'Le Praz de Lys' (D328) near the Pont des Gets, and climb to that ski resort situated on a high plateau. Carry on past the main part of Le Praz de Lys and park in a very wide area of road opposite a bar/restaurant just as the road bends to the right and begins to climb towards the Col de la Ramaz.

The Walk

There are several paths on the hillside above where you have parked. Follow the signposted path to Chalet de Véran which climbs fairly steeply as a

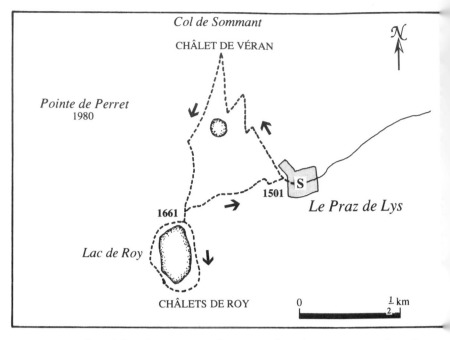

narrow path and then becomes a wider terraced track angling up to the right. At the chalet, which offers cheese for sale, turn very sharply to the left, now following a sign to 'Lac de Roy; Pic de Marcelly'. The path is narrow and can be muddy after rain, but the angle is still gentle and the hillside is rich in flowers. The rim of the basin in which the lake sits is soon reached and the adjacent peaks can be admired, their wooded slopes providing a perfect setting. The Marcelly is the highest of these mountains (*see* Walk 22).

Cross the small stream and amble round the lake on the narrow but continuous path. On returning to the rim of the basin, cross the stream to the right and look for the start of a path descending straight towards the car parking area. This path is steep and crosses stony sections but the distance is not great and most walkers will have no difficulty.

For the **Lac de Montriond walk**, take the road to the north from Morzine, following signs for Montriond or Lac de Montriond. The lake is reached in 6km (4 miles) and there is parking space near the lakeside, immediately after passing the Sapins hotel.

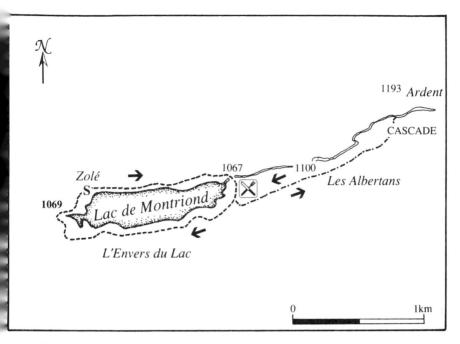

The Walk

Walk down through the trees to the lakeside and turn left on to the broad, inviting path which runs along the side of the lake, a little above water level. Across the lake is mixed woodland at the foot of precipitous cliffs. As the chalet-restaurant at the end of the lake is reached, swing right on to the broad unsurfaced roadway and then right again to return along the other shore. There is a choice here; below is a path close to the water, in all respects similar to that already followed, whilst above is a wide, easy track among the trees. Both are equally recommended.

Before returning, it is possible to extend the walk by turning left at a signpost for diversions to 'Albertans 15 minutes. Cascade 35 minutes' and following a footpath accordingly.

On returning to the near end of the lake, bear right to a bridge over the outlet stream and return to the parking area.

Walk 21   Morzine/Samoëns/Taninges: GR5/Sixt

Map no:	IGN 1:50,000: 3; Chablais, Faucigny, Genevois
Walking time:	3$^1/_2$ – 4 hours
Grading:	Moderate with one short sharp rise
Ascent:	200m (656ft)
Highest altitude:	870m (2,854ft)
Lowest altitude:	710m (2,329ft)

This is a walk of great variety. From gentle river bank to rough, almost scrambling, ascent of a steep valley side, to unspoilt agricultural hamlets. A good deal of the walk is along the long distance footpath GR5 with much of the return on very minor roads. Along the way are various interesting features and there are options for making a longer or shorter walk. Some of the ascent is on a minor road up to Les Faix hamlet, but the majority comprises a short, very sharp, rise after passing through the Les Tines gorge.

There is a good deal of off-street car parking in the middle of Samoëns.

The Walk

From the tourist information office, walk along the road to the east, towards Sixt-Fer-à-Cheval, forking right into a minor road shortly after a roundabout. A bridge over the Clevieux stream is very soon reached. Turn right before the bridge and follow the bank of the stream until two further bridges are reached. Cross either and carry on along a broad track, firstly through an area horribly despoiled by the dumping and burning of rubbish, and then generally parallel with the river Giffre, but a little way in from the bank. This is all part of GR5, which reaches a bridge over the river (the pont de Revet) in about 1$^1/_2$km (1 mile) from the scrap-burning area.

Do not cross this bridge but carry on, the track continuing very close to the edge of the river for about 1km ($^2/_3$ mile) before turning left then shortly right to follow the edge of a field, the hamlet of Sougey being in view to the left. The path joins the road at an acute angle by the old wash-house at Le Perret.

Cross the bridge, following the sign to 'Le Faix'. The red and white stripes of paint, which should now be quite familiar, are evident on the end of the bridge. Keep to the narrow road up to and through Le Faix and take the woodland track at the end of the surfaced road. On reaching a meadow, the path goes left towards the river, then right, rising in the woodland. Some walkers obviously go across the near edge of the field and rise rather steeply up a broad muddy track to cut off the corner.

In a very short distance there is a real surprise; you arrive at the entrance to a narrow defile with sheer rock on each side and no apparent exit. Carry on regardless. A flight of metal steps is provided at the far end, emerging into a jumble of rocks, through which the path winds, guided by the occasional paint marks, at the foot of a most impressive cliff face. At the end of this section, when the views open out to include the superb Fer-à-Cheval group of mountains, look for signs on a tree to the right. Almost behind the tree is one pointing to Sixt, apparently up the quite impossible precipice along the foot of which the route has already passed.

The second real surprise is that, despite the fact that the village of Sixt is clearly straight ahead, the route turns sharply right and most ingeniously climbs the valley wall, aided by another set of metal steps at the most difficult place. The way is certainly steep, and the path is narrow and in places muddy, but there is no real danger and the top is soon reached. Red arrows on a rock and a painted 'Sixt' sign ensure that the correct route is followed.

A short level section in woodland is succeeded by a steady descent towards the bank of the southern arm of the river Giffre and the hamlet of Le Fay. Cross a small meadow, the narrow path aiming between the farm buildings at the far end, and then a bridge over the river, with a disused water mill on the far side. Turn left at the mill and follow the road for $1^1/_2$km (1 mile) to Sixt, a pleasant large village shown on the maps as 'Sixt Fer-à-Cheval' but actually 'Sixt l'Abbaye' according to the roadside signs.

The return to Samoëns is entirely along surfaced roads, starting with the road along the valley for about 3km (2 miles), through the gorge to Sougey. At a wide parking area with a snack bar, divert a very short distance to the left to view the spectacular passage of the river in its deep rocky channel from a bridge. At Sougey, fork right along a minor road to Vallon d'en Haut, an unspoilt farming village with an interesting fountain on the right of the road, cut from one block of stone in 1873. A plaque on the adjacent wall commemorates the sculptor. The village of Vallon d'en Bas is next reached with its tiny chapel, built in 1636 in thanks for the village being spared the plague, when an epidemic swept the area in 1630. Both villages are exceptionally rich in timber-built houses and farm buildings, as might be

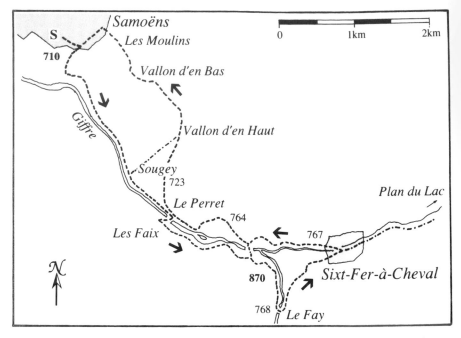

expected in a district with intense forestry and related activities. Look out for the traditional balconies, some of which have decorative carving to the woodwork. The minor road provides good walking, and a right turn in the middle of Vallon d'en Bas leads to the road between Les Moulins and Samoëns. Turn left and follow that road along the near side of the Clevieux stream to the main road. Right and then left turns will lead back to the roundabout and, a little beyond, the tourist office. Alternatively, across the main road a track along the bank of the stream leads to a bridge; turn right to return to the roundabout.

The possible variations to this walk are many. Firstly, for the shortest circuit, in just under 1km ($^1/_2$ mile) after the Revet bridge, take a track on the left heading for Vallon d'en Haut, cross the main road and continue on a minor road leading into the village. Turn left at the junction and continue as the main itinerary.

Secondly, immediately following the spectacular section through the gorge, turn sharp left opposite the signpost to 'Sixt', cross the river by a footbridge over the tremendously deep chasm, and reach the main road. Turn left to head towards Samoëns.

Thirdly, from Sixt return by bus to Samoëns. The SAT company operates a modest service along the valley. Check the timetable at any of the local tourist information offices before departure, as the service is very limited out of season .

Fourthly, for those who would prefer to walk onwards rather than back, there is a signposted path on the south side of the northern arm of the river Giffre, starting close by Sixt village centre, which leads into the wonderful *cirque* of mountains known as Fer à Cheval, reaching the picnic area at the end of the metalled road in about $6^1/_2$km (just over 4 miles). In addition to restaurants, there is an exhibition and display centre and a large area where the public may wander at will. In season some of the buses terminate here instead of at Sixt village and it should be possible to ride back to Samoëns.

Walk 22   Morzine/Samoëns/Taninges: Le Marcelly 1,999m (6,558ft)

Map no:	IGN 1:50,000: 3; Chablais, Faucigny, Genevois
Walking time:	$3^1/_2$ hours
Grading:	Experienced with some mountain walking
Ascent:	600m (1,969ft)
Highest altitude:	1,999m (6,558ft)
Lowest altitude:	1,399m (4,589ft)

Viewed from the south, the Pic de Marcelly has an elegant shape, with a large cross just visible on top. It dominates the small town of Taninges and this side of the mountain is formidably steep. Fortunately, the north side is more accessible and the peak is, in fact, the highest point on a long curving ridge. In whole or in part this ridge makes a superb high-level walk. Whilst a little care is required, walkers with any experience of mountains will find no danger or difficulty in the route described.

The starting point is the ski resort of Le Praz de Lys situated on a high plateau to the north of Taninges. From the Morzine to Taninges road (D902), it is well signposted near the Pont des Gets. A good road climbs steadily to the plateau, which is at a height of 1,400 to 1,500m (4,592 to 4,920ft). On entering Le Praz, carry on towards the main part of the resort, but turn left before reaching the commercial area, heading for the Travaillon and Tacconez restaurants. There is limited parking near to a telephone kiosk, with a larger space a little further back along the road.

The Walk

A small sign indicates 'Le Marcelly. Le Planey'. Follow the metalled road towards Le Marcelly, go straight on at a junction, to reach another post with many signs, and follow 'Le Marcelly'. Very shortly a track angles up from the road to the right, signposted to 'Pic du Marcelly. Le Planey'. Follow this, very shortly reaching a wider track, then bear left and rise steadily above the chalet

116

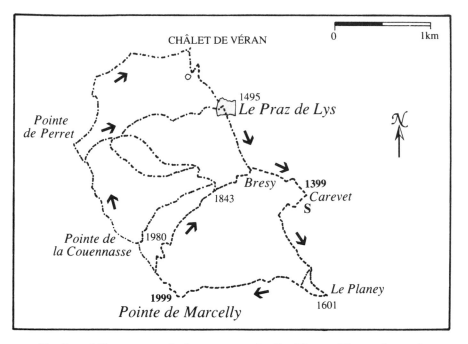

CHÂLET DE VÉRAN

0   1km

1495

Le Praz de Lys

Pointe
de Perret

Pointe
de Perret

N

Bresy   1399

1843   Carevet
                     S

Pointe de   1980
la Couennasse

1999   Le Planey
Pointe de Marcelly   1601

of Le Grand Planey towards the minor peak of Le Planey. The track is wide, the gradient easy and much of the way is along the edge of woodland. The rounded top of Le Planey is soon reached. Its position on the end of the ridge makes for a good viewpoint despite its inferior height. From Le Planey set off along the ridge, heading for Le Marcelly. A wide track leads gently downwards to a shallow col, above Le Grand Planey chalet.

There is then a short sharp rise and the Marcelly ridge begins in earnest. There can be no doubt about the route, although red paint marks do reassure from time to time. The ridge rises steadily and becomes quite narrow in places, but there are no difficulties and average walkers will not feel in any way insecure. In short, it is an absolute delight for those who like to walk in high places, with superb views to either side and glimpses of the peak looming ever larger in front.

The summit pyramid is steeper, but not particularly difficult and, at the cross, one of the best viewpoints of the central part of Haute-Savoie has been achieved. Views near and far, including Mont Blanc, are equally impressive, and the town of Taninges, with its lake, is set out like a map immediately below.

Leave the summit by the path leading along the ridge to the north. About half-way between Le Marcelly and the next peak, the Pointe de la Couennasse,

The summit ridge of Le Marcelly

turn right on to a path which descends steeply, largely in zigzags, until it becomes much more gradual, terracing across the hillside and heading for the part of Le Praz de Lys shown on the map as 'Bresy'. There are more zigzags before the track ends. From Bresy return by trackway to the parking place in a little less than 1km ($^1/_2$ mile).

There are several possible variations, either reducing or increasing this circuit. To omit the summit of Le Planey, fork right near the Grand Planey chalet on a path leading directly to the col. To extend the walk, carry on along the ridge to the next peak, Pointe de la Couennasse 1,980m (6,496ft).

From this peak a path descends to the right, joining the Marcelly descent path close to Bresy. For an even longer walk, keep going along the ridge almost to the Pointe du Perret 1,941m (6,368ft) before descending to the right, with the track forking to pass either to the north or south of the Lac de Roy, as desired. The south variant will, with a right turn at the Chalet du Roy, end yet again at Bresy, whilst the north variant will use the descent described in Walk 20 (the Lac de Roy route) to the Col de Ramaz end of Les Praz de Lys, by the bar/restaurant Chez Jean de la Pipe. The return to the starting point from here is almost 2km (a little more than 1 mile). Those who have the time and energy can complete the whole ridge by carrying on round to the Pointe de Véran 1,892m (6,207ft), descending to the Chalet de Véran, and then using the ascent path to Walk 20 (Lac de Roy) in reverse to reach Chez Jean de la Pipe.

Walk 23 Morzine/Samoëns/Taninges: Mathonex-Cessonex and Lac aux Dames/Bois de St Esprit

Map no:	(a) & (b) IGN 1:50,000: 3; Chablais, Faucigny, Genevois
Walking time:	(a) 1 hour (b) $1^1/_2$ hours
Grading:	(a) Easy with one ascent (b) Easy
Ascent:	(a) 117m (384ft) (b) None
Highest altitude:	(a) 1,000m (3,280ft) (b) 690m (2,263ft)
Lowest altitude:	(a) 883m (2,896ft) (b) 680m (2,230ft)

Two walks in one! Both are short, quite close to Samoëns and are, to a large extent, complementary. The first is a circuit based on a typical unspoilt, non-tourist, farming hamlet. It is well up the valley side and has excellent views of the valley below and nearby mountains. The second, in complete contrast, is a valley bottom walk with absolutely no ascent, partially alongside the river Giffre, the two recreational lakes 'aux dames' and within a good deal of publicly-owned forest. The Mathonex-Cessonex walk can be walked comfortably in less than 1 hour. The Lac aux Dames walk requires about $1^1/_2$ hours for the full circuit but a reduced version provides a $^3/_4$-hour walk.

For the **Mathonex-Cessonex walk**, drive to the hamlet of Mathonex. From Samoëns take the road to Morzine (summer only) (D354) which climbs eventually to the Col de Joux Plane. About 2km ($1^1/_2$ miles) from Samoëns, fork left for Plan Praz and Mathonex. From Taninges, take the Samoëns road (D907). After passing through Verchaix Gare, look for a left turn in less than 1km ($^1/_2$ mile), leading to Le Villard, and carry on up the hillside to Mathonex. There is no organised car park in Mathonex, but odd roadside areas, particularly below the chapel, can be used.

The Walk

From the chapel, walk down the road a short distance and turn left into a road

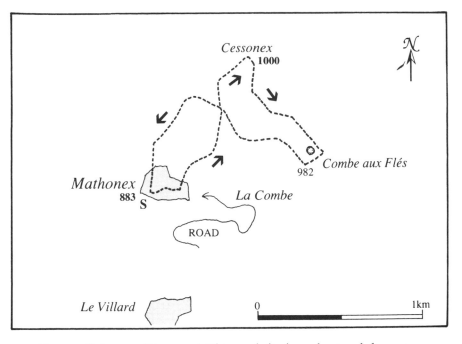

with a small signpost 'Cessonex'. This road climbs and swings left, passing a small wooden granary building on the right, lifted on blocks to exclude vermin. Pass more agricultural buildings as the road ends, becoming a grassy track. Fork left just before the beehives, following a post on a tree signed to 'Clos Piton'. The track climbs quite steeply in the form of a lane between old hedgerows, to reach the farmstead of Clos Piton and a metalled road. Keep straight on, then veer right to follow a narrow footpath which cuts across a bend in the road.

Go straight across the road into a track with a sign for 'Clos Parchet' and continue uphill by the side of a small stream. On reaching Clos Parchet turn right on to the farm access road and reach the surfaced road to Cessonex in a few metres. The hamlet with good traditional farm buildings lies to the left. Turn right for the return to Mathonex and follow the road downhill. Turn right at the first junction into a narrower road, signposted 'Mathonex and La Combe'. Perhaps unusually, this road is largely traffic-free and is a pleasure to walk, and it does have the advantage that the views can be admired without risk of falling over, which is always a hazard on a rough path.

The views include the Criou above Samoëns, and, a little further, some of the peaks of the Fer-à-Cheval. Longer views include part of the Mont Blanc *massif*. The roadside meadows are a revelation to those accustomed to the

British agricultural industry. When not under snow they are carpeted with a variety of colourful wild flowers, adding much to the attraction of Alpine rambling.

You will pass a sign giving the altitude of 1,000m (3,281ft) on the left. At the following junction, carry straight on and return to the chapel at Mathonex.

Before leaving the hamlet, look for a small oratory at the roadside below the chapel and translate the inscription for yourself. Also in Mathonex is an ancient wooden cross, from a former chapel, now fixed to the wall of the wash-house building.

For the **Lac aux Dames walk**, leave the centre of Samoëns by the straight tree-lined road heading south to the bridge over the river Giffre, and signposted to Les Saix. Just before the bridge, turn right by the entrance to the camping site; cars may be parked near the tennis courts in 300m or so.

The Walk

Walk along the track between the Lac des Dames and the camping site, cross a wooden bridge, and reach a track which runs along the top of the flooding

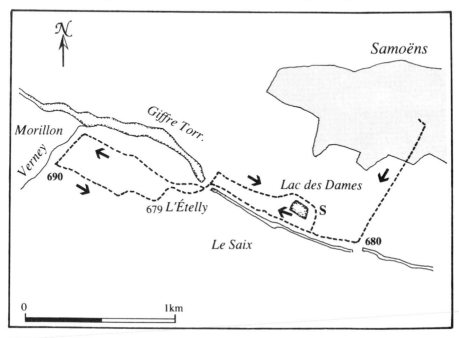

defence wall of the river Giffre. Where an access roadway leading to gravel workings crosses the route, either carry on along the wall or veer a little to the right to follow a forest track. If the latter route is chosen, fork left at the first opportunity and traverse part of a *parcours sportif*. In either case carry on to reach a long wooden footbridge over the river. This bridge is probably the best viewpoint on the walk, with the Pic du Marcelly in one direction and some of the Fer-à-Cheval group of mountains in the other direction, being well framed by the trees on either side of the river.

Cross the bridge and take the right-hand fork, bearing right again at the next junction and crossing a stony road and two small streams. On reaching the Verney stream, turn left for 50m and then left again, crossing a clearing, either directly or along the edge of the woods. Cross a small stream, follow an unsurfaced road for 100m, cross the second stream and immediately turn right for 100m, to regain the track to the river bridge. Cross the bridge.

Take the track which goes straight ahead. This is a long-distance ski route which winds through a natural grove of young conifers before reaching, on the left, an area with a rich variety of deciduous trees, some of which are named – beech, oak, ash, maple, rowan, elm and lime. Bear left to pass the lakes and return to the starting point.

For a shorter version, admire the view from the middle of the bridge and then take the return route described above.

Walk 24   Morzine/Samoëns/Taninges: La Bourgeoise – 1,770m (5,807ft)

Map no:	IGN 1:50,000: 3; Chablais, Faucigny, Genevois
Walking time:	$2^1/_2$ hours
Grading:	Moderate with some mountain walking
Ascent:	490m (1,608ft)
Highest altitude:	1,770m (5,807ft)
Lowest altitude:	1,280m (4,199ft)

La Bourgeoise is a modest mountain situated a few miles to the north of Samoëns. It has no particular significance, strategic or otherwise, but it does make a good walk from the road to the Joux Plane col and, like so many mountains of middling height, it is a superb viewpoint. The route described is largely on narrow but reliable paths, and there are no difficulties of route or potentially dangerous sections. There is a possible extension of the walk for those who are happy to walk on minor roads.

The road from Samoëns to Morzine (D364), open in summer only, is quite minor and crosses a high pass – the Col de Joux Plane. The starting point of this walk is close to the farmstead of Combe Emeru, well on the Samoëns side of the summit. From Taninges, a short cut through le Villard and Planpraz will avoid passing through Samoëns.

There are two or three roadside parking places within 300m or so of Combe Emeru, on the uphill side.

The Walk

Start by walking up the road for about $1^1/_2$km (1 mile). There is usually little traffic and the walking is not unpleasant. Pass the chalet Sur les Chables (Alt. 1,350m (4,320ft)) on the left, and, at a zigzag, where the view to the right up the valley of the river Giffre is particularly good, take a footpath to the right signposted 'Bourgeoise'. This path is narrow and ascends steeply through the woods, with the usual bilberry plants in profusion. It cuts off a large bend in

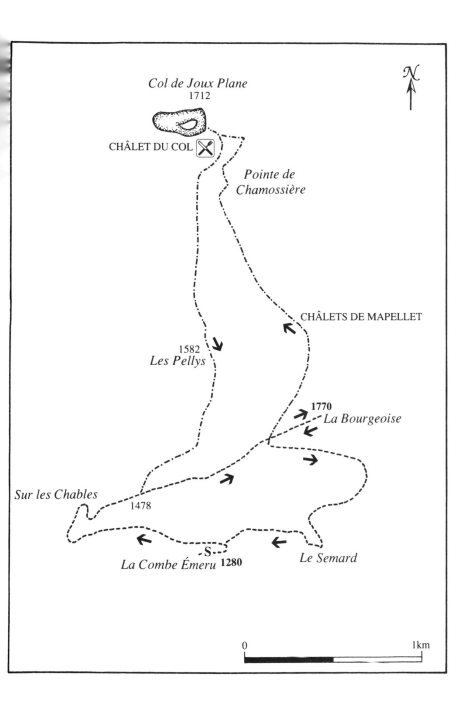

Col de Joux Plane
1712

CHÂLET DU COL

Pointe de
Chamossière

CHÂLETS DE MAPELLET

1582
Les Pellys

1770
La Bourgeoise

Sur les Chables

1478

La Combe Émeru 1280

Le Semard

N

0   1km

the road, which is soon regained. Proceed straight across the road into a footpath directly opposite, signposted 'La Bourgeoise par l'arête'. Do not be put off by *l'arête*. There is no knife-edged rocky ridge ahead with terrifying precipices and walkers hanging on by their boot laces. The route is entirely safe. It does, however, rise steeply, soon passing a take-off ramp and wind-sock for paragliding enthusiasts, another 'Bourgeoise' sign, and a seat. You will reach open ground and, shortly before the summit, there is a junction of paths: carry straight on to reach the top, which is marked by a cross, la Croix de Mapelet. The summit is not particularly exciting but the view is remarkable, even by Alpine standards. First and foremost is, inevitably, Mont Blanc. The main peak, the Aiguille du Midi and many other sharply pointed Aiguilles are all clearly visible. A little nearer, the Aiguilles Rouges and the Tête à l'Ane (Donkey's Head) are prominent, whilst, even closer at hand and to the west, are the mountains encircling the ski resort of Praz-de-Lys, Le Marcelly at one extreme and the Roc d'Enfer at the other.

You can return by descending to the signpost already mentioned and turn left following the Samoëns signpost, down a narrow path bearing left across the hillside. The descent becomes steeper and the path is very narrow indeed, marked by an occasional sign pointing upwards to 'La Bourgeoise' and splashes of yellow paint on rocks. It often seems to be heading in the wrong direction but then swings right again, through woodland and open areas, always well below the south-facing cliffs, above which the ascent path runs. Immediately following another 'Bourgeoise' sign on a tree to the left, turn sharp right into a wide unsurfaced track which passes the Chalets du Semar before joining the road. Turn left to return to the parking place.

For a longer walk, turn right on descending from the peak and follow a track which contours across the hillside, passes the Chalets de Mapelet, and reaches the road by the side of the col. This is a very attractive place, particularly at quiet times, when the adjacent restaurant is closed and the squawking of the mallard on the lake is the only sound. The return has to be along the road, but it is, after all, a minor road, all downhill, and with the open views to the south.

Walk 25   Thonon/Evian/Abondance: Mont Chauffé Circuit

Map no:	IGN 1:50,0000: 3; Chablais, Faucigny, Genevois
Walking time:	5 hours
Grading:	Experienced
Ascent:	960m (3,150ft)
Highest altitude:	1,286m (4,218ft)
Lowest altitude:	1,144m (3,752ft)

Most walkers have heard of the Tour de Mont Blanc – a long slog around Europe's highest and grandest mountain taking anything from eight to twelve or more days. Well, here is a more modest but much more original achievement – the Tour de Mont Chauffé – not quite so well known, but with a very distinct character. Its most obvious attribute is the total inaccessibility of its summit to walkers. Having accepted that fact, the prospect of circumnavigation becomes more appealing. The summit is an unusual shape; it appears to be a very narrow ridge, continuing at a fairly even height for about 3km (2 miles), with great precipices on both long sides. The paths involved in the circuit vary greatly, from gentle cart-track to one section of steep and narrow path calling for a steady head. Route-finding is not too difficult but there is ascent totalling 960m (3,150ft) which comes in three sections; going round a mountain, as opposed to a straightforward ascent, does mean a series of ups and downs. Most walkers will need about 5 hours' walking time for the circuit as described but possible variations will be suggested.

The circuit can most conveniently be started at Ubine or Le Mont, above Abondance. The main road along the Abondance valley is the D22, easily reached from Thonon or Evian by the D902, which heads up the Dranse Valley from Thonon. From Evian there is a shorter route over the hills, reaching the Abondance valley at Chevenoz. Head up the valley and, turn left for Ubine about 1½km (1 mile) after Vacheresse. For le Mont, turn left

127

at Abondance village. This turning is very tricky, because you must go up by the near side of the abbey/*mairie* and through a narrow arch. Le Mont is 2km (1^1/$_2$ miles) up the road. Parking space is plentiful at Ubine, but at Le Mont comprises only odd narrow roadside pull-offs.

The Walk

From Le Mont, commencing at the road junction with the sign 'Le Mont 1,150 metres', head up the surfaced road towards La Raille par le Sauvage. At the next chalet, the road loses its surface, soon passing another chalet and entering light woodland. At a signposted junction keep straight on. A little after the junction, a footpath is evident on the left, heading straight for the foot of the Mont Chauffé precipices. This is the start of a very 'sporting' detour, recommended only for those who insist on intimate involvement with the heart of the mountain. The detour crosses some very rugged terrain indeed and climbs very high on the mountain before descending to rejoin the main route just short of the Chalet de la Raille.

Back on course, a sign on the left indicates 1,300m (4,264ft) altitude; follow the posting to La Raille, swinging sharply to the right at a small levelled area. It is possible to short-cut to La Raille by going straight up the obvious stony slope in front, but the main track is a pleasure to walk and has much superior views. You will reach a chalet (le Crebin) and the track bends left, still rising. Pass another chalet and reach the Chalet de la Raille, with a large wooden cross outside. Ahead is a gentle rise across a meadow covered with gentians to an apparent summit. However, a short diversion will reveal that a true summit at 1,634m (5,361ft) lies nearly 400m further on.

The main route is along a path to be found 30m beyond the cross. The nature of the walking is now about to change. The route to La Raille is so good and easy that it is worth doing in its own right. The new path starts off quite well, descending gently across a hillside. On reaching a small valley it turns right, downhill, for some distance before bearing left and emerging at the top of a fearsomely steep hillside, down which it plunges in zigzags, in places on mud, which is slippery after rain. High up there are one or two distinctly exposed sections, but it does improve lower down.

Just before the stream, join a wide, well-used track and turn left, uphill. This is part of the Portes du Soleil long-distance footpath and is marked by red triangles. On reaching a signpost, there is a choice of route. The Portes du Soleil path swings right and then left to reach the next objective, the Col d'Ubine, whilst a steep narrow track makes straight for the obvious col on the skyline. The direct route is steep but not difficult and is easy enough to follow

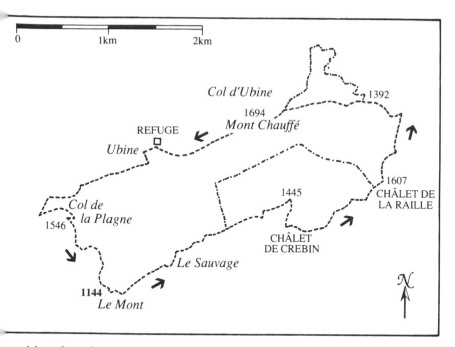

although it does divide in places. The track runs close to the northern precipice of Mont Chauffé, which is even more impressive than that on the south, a sheer rock wall providing nesting places for a fair number of birds. The col is reached in 35–45 minutes, with its signpost '1693 metres'; carry on here, following the sign for Chalets d'Ubine, which are clearly visible ahead. The descent is slight and the walk along a minor path (which is, once again, the Portes du Soleil route) in a wide mountain valley is pleasant. Ubine is a small hamlet which has road access, a chapel and a refuge. Before the chapel, look for a track on the left, dropping a little to cross the stream and then rising steadily on the flank of the hillside opposite, before entering woodland. Quite soon, the view across the Abondance valley opens up as a high pasture is reached before dropping gently to the Col de la Plagne du Mont, 1,546m (5,071ft), with its cross and signpost. From the col a rough stony roadway leads down towards Le Mont and Abondance. For the shortest return look for a path on the right in about 300m, which goes directly to Le Mont. The roadway carries on to join the Le Mont to La Raille road along which the walk started. If this descent is used, turn right at the junction to return to Le Mont, looking out for squirrels in the woodland.

Should the circuit be started at Ubine, the chapel makes an obvious

The Col d'Ubine and the north face of Mont Chauffé

starting place and the traverse of the Col de la Plagne becomes the first section. For those who can read directions backwards there is no good reason why Mont Chauffé should not be circumnavigated in a clockwise direction!

Walk 26 Thonon/Evian/Abondance: Lac des Plagnes and Abondance Circular

Map no:	(a) & (b) IGN 1:50,000: 3; Chablais, Faucigny, Genevois
Walking time:	(a) 1 hour (b) $2^1/_2$ hours
Grading:	(a) Easy (b) Easy to moderate
Ascent:	(a) 95m (312ft) (b) 301m (987ft)
Highest altitude:	(a) 1,286m (4,218ft) (b) 1,210m (3,969ft)
Lowest altitude:	(a) 1,191m (3,906ft) (b) 909m (2,982ft)

This pair of walks is based on Abondance. Both are entirely without difficulty and, although there is ascent in both cases, the going is generally easy, using a fair amount of minor road in the case of the Abondance circular. The Lac des Plagnes is quite small but has a pleasant, partially wooded setting with hills rising steeply behind. It is a good place for a family picnic, as the shore is readily accessible. The Abondance walk passes through woodland and amongst Alpine agriculture, with good views across the valley.

The **Lac des Plagnes** is reached in about 6km (4 miles) by a minor road to the south from Abondance, forking left above the main village square. There is a large, rough parking area adjacent to the small St Anne's chapel.

The Walk

Start by walking up the unsurfaced road above the parking area, rising steadily with good views over the lake. You will reach a junction, where you bear right, towards the Chalet de Tinderets, to reach a fine mountain amphitheatre with a chalet on the right and a bridge over the stream ahead. For the return, head back a few metres and, at an area where cars may be parked, look for a '40' painted in red on a white ground on a rock. A small path will be found, plunging steeply down the hillside. There is a side-track for a few metres to view a waterfall, which can also be seen to advantage from lower down. The path may be slippery after rain but is easy to follow and soon

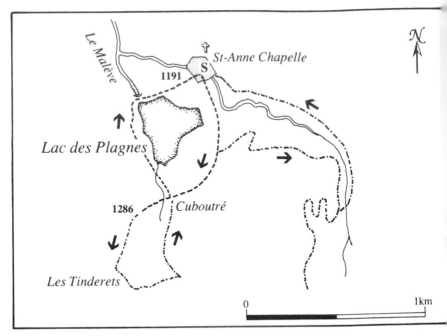

reaches a plank bridge over the stream a little below the waterfall. Cross the bridge and carry on to join a wider path, bearing left and emerging from the woodland with a splendid view of the lake. The lakeside path is joined and is followed round the end of the lake to return to the parking area.

There are possible variations. Those who want the most gentle walk possible can encircle the lake, whilst a longer walk can be achieved in two ways. Firstly, by turning left at the signposted junction towards the Chalets de Lens and following that unsurfaced roadway until, at the end of a zigzag, a path branches off on the left, crosses the stream, and swings round to the left descending back to the chapel in parallel with the stream.

Secondly, having reached the amphitheatre-like valley, it is possible to achieve a low-level circuit before returning to the lake.

For the second walk, there is plenty of car parking space in Abondance village and there is also a bus service up and down the valley.

The Walk

From the central area, take the road uphill, bearing right towards Frogy and Prétairié. Pass the base of the ski-lift and a pond with a shrine, crossing the

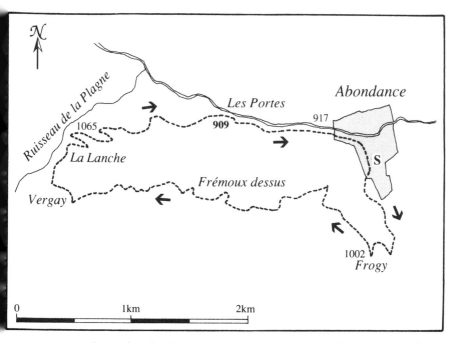

stream twice. Immediately after the second crossing, fork right for the small
hamlet of Frogy with its chalets so typical of this particular Alpine valley.
Follow the minor road, largely free of traffic as it winds uphill, with good views
over the Abondance valley. As the road loses its surface and bends sharply
to the left, just above a farm complex, cross the stream and then turn right
at a signpost for 'Fremoux 1,180 metres; Chalets de l'Essert; Les Portes' and
follow the broad track rising through the woodland.

The track emerges from woodland close to a large chalet and carries on to
reach a minor col above another chalet, with a signpost 'Fremoux Dessus'.
Follow the signposting towards Les Portes to the right, being careful not to
take the very obvious forestry roadway by mistake. The correct route is
slightly downhill from the signpost and soon becomes a wide unsurfaced
roadway through the forest, falling gently for the most part. Some sections
may be churned by tractors and animals and be a little unpleasant in wet
weather.

In a little under 1¹/₂km (1 mile) a chalet is reached to the right of the track.
Fork right across a small pasture, heading for the chalet, where another
signpost confirms the route to Les Portes. Proceed more steeply down the
rough roadway ahead to a large chalet (La Lanche), where a surfaced road is
reached. Follow this down its zigzags, looking carefully for an even more

The abbatical church, Abondance

minor road on the right to cut off a corner. If that turning is missed, the stream is crossed twice on the road before heading straight for Les Portes (the junction between the minor road and the main valley road), via Les Granges.

From Les Portes junction, with its stone cross and 910m (2,985ft) altitude, turn right and follow the valley road back to Abondance, forking right by the tennis courts, to reach the village centre.

Walk 27 Thonon/Evian/Abondance: Lac de Tavaneuse

Map no:	IGN 1:50,000: 3; Chablais, Faucigny, Genevois
Walking time:	3½ hours
Grading:	Moderate with a steep ascent and descent
Ascent:	760m (2,493ft)
Highest altitude:	1,890m (6,199ft)
Lowest altitude:	1,130m (3,706ft)

The lake is the principal objective of this walk. It is, however, set high in the mountains, cradled by steep slopes, like an English lakeland tarn. Both ascent and descent are steep and rough but are without danger. Presumably because motor vehicles, even those of 4-wheel drive with local drivers, cannot approach the lake from any direction, it is a place of peace and calm, with an atmosphere of remoteness. For those who love mountains this is sufficient reward for the long ascent, totalling 760m (2,493ft), including the short climb after the lake.

There are several possible variations to the circuit described below.

From Abondance, take the minor road to the south, forking right just above the main square, to head for Prétairié. As this minor road peters out, there is ample car parking space on rough ground.

The Walk

A signpost near the access to the parking area points the way up to the Lac de Tavaneuse. Walk through the parking area and carry on up a wide stony track until a sign is reached at a parting of the ways. Turn left for the lake, cross a stream, and start the real ascent on a steep mountain track. At a T-junction, bear left and, at a subsequent fork, bear right. Although the going is steep and rough, the route is never in doubt. As happens not infrequently on mountain ascents, the top appears to be just in front on two or three occasions, only for hopes to be dashed by yet another hillside appearing just above the apparent

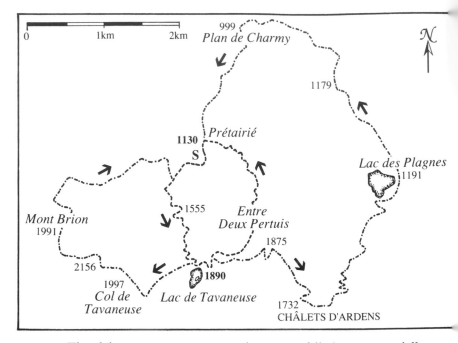

crest. This delusion is most pronounced as a waterfall plunges over cliffs on the left; surely the lake must sit in the basin obviously drained by that stream? Unfortunately, this is not so; on emerging into the basin by a chalet, the walker is confronted by a steep hillside opposite over which the path continues to climb. At the top of this slope, the lake is reached, the signpost claiming 1,800m (5,905ft) altitude, as against the 1,805m (5,922ft) of the IGN map.

The return commences with another climb. Take the minor path signposted 'entre deux Perthuis' and 'Chalets d'Ardens' and ascend to a mini-col above the lake, with another signpost. As the track divides, bear left, heading for the clearly visible Chalets d'entre deux Perthuis situated at the lip of a wide mountain valley.

From the chalets the long descent to Prétairié is by the access track to the chalets; it is steep and often muddy, but twists and turns skilfully to avoid any danger on this steep mountainside. By this track, men and beasts have for generations been able to reach these incredibly inaccessible chalets in order to use the summer grazing. There are no signposts, no paint marks on the rocks, but the way is never in doubt, particularly if there has been recent movement of stock up or down, leaving much of the surface well churned.

Eventually, the path emerges from woodland into open meadow, heading

Lac de Tavaneuse

for a chalet, beyond which is a plank bridge over a stream and the Prétairié road. Turn left to the parking area.

From the lake, other return routes are possible, including, of course, a return by the ascent path. A longer walk results from forking right just after the mini-col above the lake, following the sign 'Chalets d'Ardens', crossing the slope well below the rocky summit, climbing the shoulder opposite, and following an up and down high level route before swinging left for the long descent to Lac des Plagnes (*see* Walk 26). From the lake it is about 4km ($2^1/_2$ miles) down the road to a left turn which connects with the road from

Abondance to Prétairié. For this circuit, cars could be parked closer to the road junction to even out the walking on the roads.

Another long walk option is to take the path from the lake to the Col de Tavaneuse, 1,997m (6,550ft) then turn right to climb to the ridge which includes five separate mountain summits – the first, in just over 2km ($1^1/_2$ miles), is the highest – at 2,156m (7,073ft). After this you bear right to descend steeply towards Prétairié. Much of this route is regarded as difficult and is definitely only for experienced mountain walkers.

Walk 28   Thonon/Evian/Abondance: Balcon du Léman – Mont d'Hermone

Map no:	IGN 1:50,000: 3; Chablais, Faucigny, Genevois
Walking time:	$2^1/_2$ hours
Grading:	Moderate
Ascent:	293m (961ft)
Highest altitude:	1,413m (4,635ft)
Lowest altitude:	1,120m (3,674ft)

The Balcon du Léman is a long distance footpath following the line of the southern shore of the huge Lac Léman, but at a distance of several kilometres. The *balcon*, in order to achieve its objective of providing a walk giving more or less continuous views over the lake, is generally on high ground. It travels along the crest of the Alpine foothills which rise attractively at a short distance from the lake shore behind Thonon and Evian, and right from the lake shore further east, towards the Swiss frontier. The Mont d'Hermone is one such foothill. It is a long, narrow hill, well wooded, and with the *balcon* path along its crest. It is pleasant to walk with a good track and no route-finding problems. From the Col du Feu, the possible variations are considerable. As a guide, an out and back excursion to the church of Notre Dame d'Hermone involves ascent of 206m (676ft) and a walking time of $1^1/_4$ hours.

To reach the Col du Feu from Thonon or Evian, take the D903 towards Annemasse, and fork left to reach Noyer, Orcier, and then ascend the col. From Abondance, the col is approached from its other side, via the valley road, La Vernaz, Chez Marphoz, Vailly and Lulin. There is a large parking area at the col, opposite the bar/restaurant.

The Walk

Set off up the surfaced road to the left of the restaurant, following the signpost 'Notre Dame d'Hermone par Le Feu 45 minutes'. This road is part of the

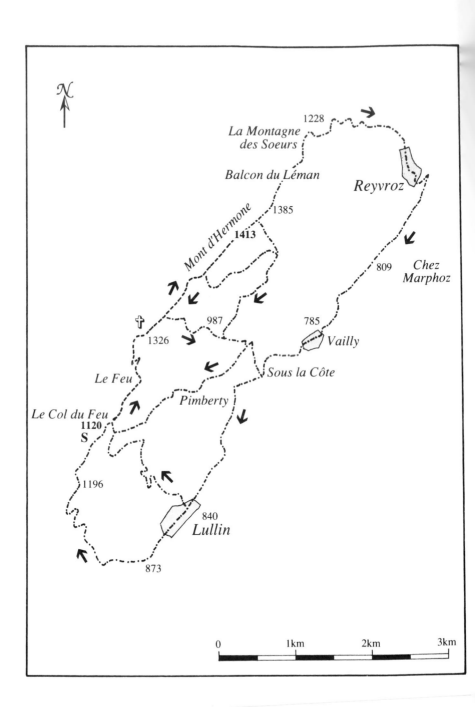

N

1228
La Montagne
des Soeurs

Balcon du Léman

Reyvroz

Mont d'Hermone
1385

1413

809
Chez
Marphoz

987
1326

785
Vailly

Le Feu

Sous la Côte

Pimberty

Le Col du Feu
1120
S

1196

840
Lullin

873

0   1km   2km   3km

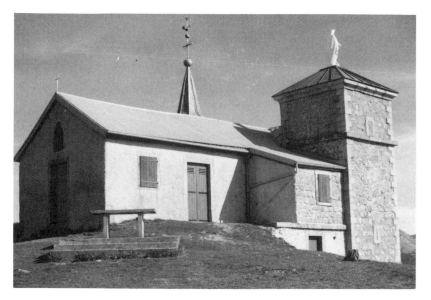

The chapel of Notre-Dame d'Hermone

Balcon du Léman path, and soon loses its surface, which is regained before reaching the hamlet of Le Feu. Keep left at a junction, pass a farmstead and, as the road finally loses its surface, climb quite steeply, passing a sign that is just legible, 'Hermone'. The path continues to rise and reaches a section with the stations of the cross depicted by small statues on pedestals along the way. These lead, seemingly inevitably, to the chapel of Notre Dame d'Hermone, perched on a knoll at 1,326m (4,350ft), and making a wonderful viewpoint in all directions.

The track carries on along the ridge, with red and white paint markings to confirm the route. As the highest point of Mont Hermone lies about $1^1/_2$km (1 mile) ahead, there is still some ascent. The path remains good and there are sufficient breaks in the tree screen to allow views on one side or the other. Tracks downhill to the right are passed in three places, as the *balcon* carries on towards Reyvroz.

Having reached the highest point, which is not in any way marked as a summit, there are several possibilities. A straightforward return allows the balcon to be enjoyed in both directions, with a walking time of approximately $2^1/_2$ hours.

Alternatively, the full length of Mont Hermone, and La Montagne des Soeurs can be walked, ending at Reyvroz. This means a long return walk on minor roads, via Chez Marphoz, Vailly and Lulin (which can be avoided on a short-cut path), unless transport can be arranged at Reyvroz.

Shorter circular walks can be achieved by turning right at any of the three signposted junctions along the *balcon*. From the first, Le Plansuet is soon reached, with a track leading to the zigzagging road descending to Sous la Côte. Return to the col either via Lulin and the minor road or via Pimberty and a short-cutting footpath reaching the road a little below the col.

The second and third right turns descend to Les Combes. After Les Combes, make for the minor road by bearing left and then right, and follow the zigzags down to Sous la Côte, as suggested above.

Walk 29 Thonon/Evian/Abondance: Lac Léman/La Châtaigneraie and L'Ermitage Forest

Map no:	(a) & (b) IGN 1:50,000: 3; Chablais, Faucigny, Genevois
Walking time:	(a) 2 hours (b) flexible
Grading:	(a) & (b) Easy
Ascent:	(a) & (b) Not significant
Highest altitude:	(a) 390m (1,279ft) (b) 620m (2,034ft)
Lower altitude:	(a) 380m (1,246ft) (b) 560m (1,837ft)

These two shorter walks are particularly recommended because of their ready accessibility from Thonon. Both are very easy strolls; ascent is nil in the case of the walk along the Lac Léman shore and not really significant in the case of L'Ermitage forest. There the resemblance ends. The great attraction of the lake walk is the lake shore itself and the views across the water, followed by the Châtaigneraie public recreation area and a possible visit to the Château de Ripaille. The second walk, on the other hand, is purely and simply forest walking, with sufficient variety in the tree types and in the rise and fall and general shaping of the landscape to maintain interest. There is, however, one other common feature; each route has an organised exercise course for those whose energies exceed the requirements of the walk.

For the **Lac Léman walk**, there is a fair amount of car parking in the centre of Thonon, most of it requiring payment. Alternatively, there are good free parking areas close to the Port de Rives, down at the lakeside.

The Walk

From the town centre take the funicular railway to descend to the port or, alternatively, walk down through the attractive cliff gardens. Opposite the base of the funicular is the port. Turn right along the Quai de Rives and continue along the Quai de Ripaille, a wide lakeside promenade, bedecked with flowers. As the road swings to the right, the promenade ends at the

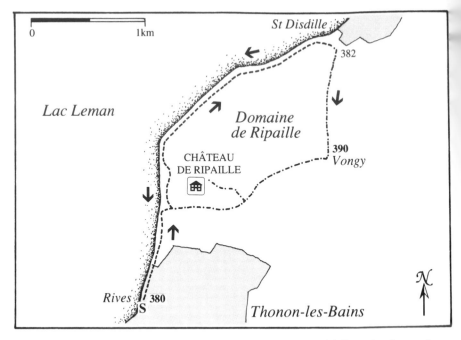

entrance to the municipal beach. Go up the steps, and follow the footpath beside the road for a short distance, to the end of the beach boundary fence. Turn left into a wide, splayed, access just before reaching the Château de Ripaille, which can be seen to the right. Except for nomads and campers, the route lies straight ahead, with the château vineyards on the right. The signboard reads 'Littoral du Léman. St Disdille 35 minutes. Vongy 1 hour 10 minutes'. The path is initially metalled, but soon becomes unsurfaced and reaches the edge of the lake. All the way to St Disdille, the track lies between the lake and the great wall which encloses the grounds of the château, the Domaine de Ripaille. Whilst the true path generally lies close to the wall, the walker is free to choose a route along the lakeside shingle, giving much better views across the lake.

Eventually the wall turns sharply right and the Châtaigneraie is reached. This is a public area of chestnut and other trees, 5 hectares (12$^1/_2$ acres) in extent, equipped with picnic tables, children's play equipment and an extensive CRAPA course (*circuit rustique d'activités physiques aménagé*). Keep to the shore of the lake to reach the St Disdille beach towards the far end of the Châtaigneraie. Port Ripaille is a little further in the same direction, reachable by road.

The return can be along the same path or along the two roads which flank the château grounds on the landward side. There is a summer bus service. On reaching the car park by the château entrance, a trip on the 'little train' (in season only) is an alternative for the return along the quays to Port Rives. The château itself, which dates from the fifteenth century, is open to visitors every day in high season, and Sunday afternoons only out of season. Guided tours are available. For visits to the extensive forest within the château boundary, there is a side entrance on the Rue de la Forêt, with its own car park. In addition to the main forest which is 53 hectares (131 acres), there is an arboretum, commenced between 1930 and 1934, with many interesting and unusual types of tree in evidence. On sale at the château is the white wine produced from the surrounding vineyard and bottled on the premises.

For the **forest walk**, whilst it is possible to park cars in several places on the periphery of the forest, it is best to use the official area. From Thonon, take the road towards Armoy (D26) and look for a minor right turn, not far out of the built-up area, for Ermitage, and then steeply up to the left for Bois de la Cour. The parking area is soon reached on the left.

The Walk

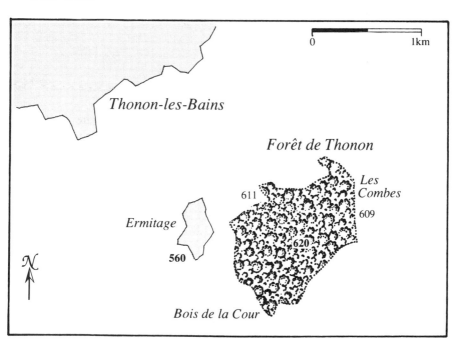

Château de Ripaille

From the parking area take a broad track which runs for 50 or 60m parallel with the minor road to reach the *plan de la forêt* – a cleared area with a large map setting out the various recommended walks.

The start of the CRAPA (*circuit rustique d'activités physiques aménagé*), which has no less than thirty-eight different exercise points in a course of 2,200m (almost $1^1/_2$ miles), is also at the *plan de la forêt*.

There are four recommended circuits, each colour-coded, ranging from 2,684m (over $1^1/_2$ miles) to 5,690m ($3^1/_2$ miles) in length. As most of the trackways are named, there is little danger of becoming lost, and there is no reason why any circuit up to about $1^1/_2$ hours duration should not be made. From the northern fringe of the forest, there are views over Thonon to the lake.

Walk 30 Thonon/Evian/Abondance: Pic Boré 1,974m (6,476ft)

Map no:	IGN 1:50,000: 3; Chablais, Faucigny, Genevois
Walking time:	$3^1/_2$ – 4 hours
Grading:	Moderate to experienced
Ascent:	923m (3,028ft)
Highest altitude:	1,974m (6,476ft)
Lowest altitude:	1,051m (3,448ft)

The Pic Boré is a prominent peak very close to the shore of Lac Léman. In fact, as the crow flies the distance is only about 4km ($2^1/_2$ miles), which makes it a superb viewpoint both for the lake and its surroundings, and for range after range of mountains, including the Diablerets across the Swiss frontier. Although it is a real mountain peak, the ascent is quite straightforward and without danger. From Lajoux, as described, the total ascent is 923m (3,028ft) taking about $2^1/_4$ or $2^1/_2$ hours, whilst the whole circuit requires $3^1/_2$ to 4 hours.

The walk starts at a junction of several roads, at the western end of Lajoux, which is 3km (2 miles) east of Thollon. Thollon is readily accessible from Thonon and Evian by the D24. An alternative from Thonon is to use the D21 via Publier and St Paul en Chablais. From Abondance, proceed by Chevenoz, then take the D32 to reach St Paul en Chablais, turning right towards Thollon. There is limited car parking space on grassy verges.

The Walk

On the south side of the road junction, a wooden signpost points the way to 'Col de Cornien and Chalets de Mémises'. Set off up the broad, unsurfaced roadway. Forty metres after passing a small chalet on the right, turn right at a signpost to Chalets de Mémises. The path is narrow and ascends steeply between young coniferous trees. Parts of this track may be muddy after rain and are sufficiently steep for this to be unpleasant. It is otherwise a good track, picking its way neatly up a steep hillside and with the route confirmed by red

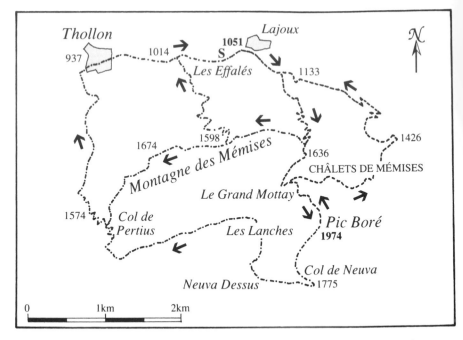

paint marks on rocks. After a little more than 1 hour the Mémise ridge is reached, with its little sign 'télécabine'. The view opens up in front, including the Pic Boré itself, straight ahead. Turn right on to a wide stony roadway, rising steadily to the next signpost; to the right is 'Pic de Mémises' whilst ahead and a little to the left towards the chalet buildings is 'Borée'.

Before reaching the buildings, swing right on to a track which starts on the level but soon rises to the left, after a junction, climbing quite steeply. Most of the tracks in this area are subject to use by vehicles involved with skiing and may be considerably churned at times. The track swings right and heads for a cabin at the top of a ski-lift.

Beyond the cabin the path is at first indistinct. However, as the rocky summit is faced, a very narrow but quite distinct path can be seen making for the wide gap between the cliffs. Follow this and you will reach the round grassy top without difficulty. Beware that a precipice lies immediately behind the summit!

The view is certainly worth lingering over. The lake, a good deal of Switzerland, the Jura, and much of the northern part of mountainous Haute-Savoie are all in view. Quite near, and lower, is the Pic de Blanchard, whilst to the south, and even nearer, is the Dent d'Oche, with the Cornettes de Bise behind to the left.

There are several options for the return journey, apart from the obvious use of the same route. All but one involve using the same descent from the actual summit. The odd one out is to descend the steep grass, with great care in wet weather, and to join the obvious track carrying on along the ridge before dropping to the Col de Neuva. At the col, turn right, and pass the chalet of Neuva Dessus. Bear right again, pass the ruins of Les Lanches and carry on to the Col de Pertuis, from which there is a steep descent to Thollon and a walk along the road to the car parking place.

Other return routes can take in one or both of the summits on the Mémises ridge, by returning past the Mémise Chalets and then turning left a little before the long descent. The first, and higher, peak, 1,686m (5,531ft) is situated half-way to the top of a descent path which follows the line of the *télécabine* lift quite closely, to arrive at the ski centre of Les Effalés. For the second peak, 1,674m (5,492ft) carry on past the hotel. The track along the Mémise ridge is part of a variant of the Balcon du Léman long distance footpath. From this peak, continue until the Col de Pertuis is reached, and turn right to return to Thollon.

For the recommended return circuit, descend past the ski-lift cabin and look for a minor track turning sharply right as the main track bends to the left. This track keeps at much the same level, firstly in the open and then in woodland. It is not very distinct in parts and walkers must resist the temptation to turn left, downhill, as gullies are crossed. The track does eventually turn left shortly before a very steep slope is reached ahead. Again, it is not very distinct in the woodland, largely due to being churned by cattle. If the steep slope is kept a little to the right, there is no danger of going badly off course. At the bottom edge of the woodland there is a signpost which, perhaps against the evidence, does prove that the last few hundred metres was a proper route after all. Turn right towards Col de Cornien, and follow a path which has paint marks of various colours on stones. Do not attempt to differentiate, there is only one real path towards the chalet which is visible below, although those who prefer may well take a route directly down the hillside. The path bends considerably to the right until, at a minor junction marked by a blue arrow on a rock, a left turn is taken leading more directly to the chalet. This not-too-distinct turning occurs just after the main track has started to rise. More splashes of blue paint may be seen on a bush and on another rock just after the junction.

On reaching the chalet carry straight on along a broad grassy ridge. About 30m before reaching woodland, look carefully for red and white marks on a tree. There is an arrow pointing to the right, where the track rakes back sharply and begins to descend. The way is confirmed by red and white

The view west from Pic Boré

markings on a larger tree. Cross a small stream and descend steeply towards an open pasture below. Part way down, there is a choice of route, as a track on the left cuts off a small corner. On reaching the meadow take a broad, forestry type track in the left-hand corner which leads to the bottom of the de la Frasse ski-lift. A few metres before reaching the lift cabin turn sharply right and follow a minor path which soon improves and broadens before rising a little to reach a sign on a tree to the right, pointing to Cornien and Novel to the right and Mémise behind. Turn left and follow a wide unsurfaced roadway, at first descending steadily towards Lac Léman. Although initially the direction appears to be wrong, this track zigzags lower down and then swings left across the apparently impassable valley to provide a very easy and *balcon*-like return to Lajoux.

APPENDICES

I Tour de Mont Blanc – Suggested 7-day itinerary

First Day

Depart from Les Houches 1,000m (3,280ft) to Bellevue (cabin-lift) and follow the variant path which heads for the Col de Tricot, 2,120m (6,954ft), passing Châlet d'Are. This variant takes the walker close to the Aiguille du Goûter, the north face of the Bionnassay, the Dômes de Miage before dropping to Les Contamines. Just beyond Les Contamines, the main route is rejoined for the walk up the valley along a famous section of pathway paved by the Romans, to reach the refuge of Nant Borrand. Purists not wishing to use the cabin-lift may commence by walking up to Bellevue by way of the Col de Voza (*see* Walk 14).

Second Day

From the Nant Borrand refuge 1,460m (4,789ft) make for the Col du Bonhomme 2,483m (8,144ft), and descend to Les Chapieux, where there is a gîte d'étape and the refuge La Nova. This part of the circuit heads a little away from the main Mont Blanc *massif*, coming closer to the Beaufortin area and with views of Mont Pourri. Chapieux is well known for its goats and their cheese.

Third Day

Leave Les Chapieux 1,554m (5,097ft) in a north-easterly direction, heading for the Col de la Seigne, 2,513m (8,243ft). At the summit of the col, the French/Italian frontier is crossed, and the south-west side of Mont Blanc is in view. The destination is the refuge Elisabetta, close to the huge Lex Blanche glacier and the Tré la Tête peaks.

Fourth Day

The refuge Elisabetta is at 2,150m (7,052ft), and the route continues to the north-east, reaching Lac de Combal 1,959m (6,426 ft) before turning south-east and then back to north-east to pass Lac Chécroui and climb the Col Chécroui. Here, either the right fork variant descending steeply to Courmayeur or the *téléphérique* may be used. From Courmayeur climb to the refuge Giorgio Bertonne on the variant route or, if time permits, continue to Levachy, where there is a choice of accommodation.

Fifth Day

From the refuge or from Levachy, 1,642m (5,386ft) head for the Grand Col Ferret, 2,537m (8,321ft) on the Italian/Swiss frontier, descend to Ferret and on to La Fouly, 1,610m (5,281ft). Catch the bus to Champex and then walk to the Châlet d'Arpette, again on a variant route. On the ascent to the frontier, note the unusual Pré de Bar glacier.

Sixth Day

From Arpette the variant climbs over the Fenêtre d'Arpette, 2,671m (8,761ft) then descends to rejoin the main route near Trient, 1,300m (4,264ft) where there are two gîtes. This is quite a difficult section, but the effort is repaid by the superb view from the summit over the Glacier du Trient.

Seventh Day

Follow the main route to the Col de Balme, 2,191m (7,186ft), crossing back into France, descend past Le Tour to Montroc and Tré les Champs, 1,417 (4,648ft) and return to Les Houches.

From Tré les Champs, the main path and the variant climb by different routes to la Flégère and continue to the Col du Brévent and Le Brévent peak before descending to Les Houches. Most walkers will seek help from the public transport along the Chamonix valley for at least some of the great distance between Trient and Les Houches.

General Information

The above itinerary enables the tour to be completed in one week, albeit with the aid of some public transport. Walkers with more time available may well end Day 4 at the refuge Giorgio Bertonne and then split Day 5 into 2 days, staying at Ferret or La Fouly on the intermediate night, and possibly ending a little shorter at Champex. Likewise, Day 7 could be split to allow time to walk the whole of the high-level part of the tour on the north-west side of the Chamonix valley. A break at Montroc or Tré les Champs would give a fairly short day from Trient, whilst carrying on to the hôtel at La Flégère would result in a much harder day, but a comparatively easy final day to Les Houches. In difficult weather the route over the Fenêtre d'Arpette is better avoided by using the main route from Champex to the Col de la Forclaz and then descending to Trient.

The refuges and other accommodation for walkers are open only during a comparatively short season, usually mid-June to mid-September. During that season they are very busy and reservation of a place is strongly advised. At some refuges reservation is essential. Meals are generally available at reasonable prices and this has the advantage of reducing the burden over this onerous route. A list of the accommodation relevant to the Tour de Mont Blanc, with name of proprietor, opening times, prices and telephone number, can be obtained from local tourist offices or from the Maison de la Montagne, 74310 Les Houches (tel: 50 54 50 76).

II Chamonix – The Natural Environment

Those who discover Chamonix and its surroundings are always filled with wonder at the perfect balance which prevails in the harmony of the landscapes which nature has created; an association of the rough world of rock and ice with the living universe of water and vegetation. Flora and fauna have an important place and depend closely upon the ecology of this Alpine environment, characterised by a cold and dry climate, abundant snowfalls, strong winds, a bitter spring and a short summer.

Two other factors must be added to these severe climatological conditions, where only well-adapted species can survive: the effects produced by the chemical composition of the ground, mostly silicious, and the north-eastern/south-western orientation of the valley, which makes its slopes so different; hot and dry on one side, cold and damp on the other. The vegetation is very specific and changes as rapidly as the altitude, and the wildlife also spreads out in distinct levels. Finally, there is also the action of the glaciers which either erode or free the soil with their backwards and forwards motion, as well as the avalanches in winter which leave gullies and ravines, where shrubs and annual plants prevail.

Among the vegetable species which constitute the flora of the upper Arve valley and the Val de Vallorcine, trees are numerous, often very tall, and make up huge forestry sites. They play a great aesthetic, economic and, especially, ecological role.

Resinous species prevail on the mountains and at lower altitudes are mixed with deciduous trees, which are smaller and with a shorter life-span. The spruce is by far the most common (seventy-five per cent of the total) and is always confused with the fir. Above 1,800m (5,904ft) it gives way to the larch, another conifer, and the only tree of the pine family which sheds its needles in winter.

At this high altitude, trees are more spaced out and their size decreases. Even higher, the larch is replaced by the *arolle* or *pin cembrot*, carrying needles grouped in fives, which, in turn, is replaced by mainly shrubs, among which are juniper, rhododendrons and dwarf willow. Above these are numerous meadows covered with an array of mountain flowers, reaching the snow and ice.

Between 1,000 and 1,500m (3,280 – 4,920ft) the walker will find the genuine fir tree, the Scotch pine and the hook fir tree. Birches, service trees and maples grow in spaces among the conifers. The white alder spreads in the valley bottom near the streams, whilst the green alder is found in the avalanche corridors. The undergrowth of small shrubs, elder and bilberries is found everywhere.

There is also a large variety of animals. As the altitude increases, successively, roe deer, stags, squirrels, martens, hazel hens, owls and buzzards are found in the spruce forest . The hare finds shelter among the larch forests, then the marmot, the chamois and the white partridge. Even higher are the ibex and the golden eagle. The fox, the badger and the ermine are found at all levels. Reptiles are few and are generally on the north-eastern slopes, but vipers are common on the south-western slopes.

The forest has a very special place in this Alpine sphere. Although apparently robust, it does suffer from the excesses of the Alpine climate. It has to regulate the rate of water-flow, neutralise the effects of pluvial erosion and limit the number and the violence of avalanches. The forest is an essential element for man, as it produces wood, encourages tourism, and plays an important role in the economic life of the valley. Four thousand hectares (9,600 acres) belong to the town and to the state. The task of the *Office National des Forêts* is to administer and to protect this precious natural heritage.

With acknowledgements to Daniel Arquillère, Technicien Forestier de l'Office National des Forêts

III Vocabulary

En route

airport	un aéroport
ticket	un billet
connection	une correspondence
fare	un prix
to take off	décoller
to smoke	fumer
to land	atterrir
boat	un bateau
cabin	une cabine
(the) deck	le pont
English Channel	la Manche
harbour	un port
man overboard	homme à la mer!
railway line	chemin de fer
mountain railway	chemin de fer de montagne
tunnel	un tunnel
station	la gare
booking office	le guichet
return journey	aller et retour
family ticket	billet de famille
first (second) class	première (deuxième) classe
day ticket	valable pour un jour
train	un train
express train	un train express (rapide)
railway coach	une voiture (wagon)
compartment (no smoking)	un compartiment (de non fumeurs)
sleeping coach	un wagon lit
motorway	autoroute
road	une route (un chemin)
priority	priorité
give way	cédez le passage
bend	un virage
verge	l'accotement
right	droite
left	gauche
cul de sac	impasse, voie sans issue

traffic	la circulation
traffic lights	les feux
no entry	sens interdit
no parking	défense de stationner
one-way traffic	circulation à sens unique
car	une voiture (auto)
bicycle	une bicyclette
lorry	un camion
motorbike	une moto
driving licence	un permis de conduire
uneven road surface	chaussée déformée
slippery road surface	chaussée glissante
brakes	les freins
lights	les phares (feux)
to light up	allumer
petrol	l'essence
coach	un autocar (car)
enquiry office	un bureau de renseignements
coach station	la gare d'autocars
booking seats	la location des places
timetable	un horaire
coach tour	un circuit en autocar
luggage	les bagages
suitcase	une valise
bag (hand)	sac (à main)
taxi	un taxi
for hire	libre
price	le prix
taxi driver	un chauffeur de taxi (conducteur)
the fare clock	le compteur (taximètre)
customs	la douane
nothing to declare	rien à déclarer
passport	le passeport

Accommodation

hotel	un hôtel
furnished apartment	appartement meublé
guest house	une pension
to rent	louer

room	une chambre
youth hostel	une auberge de la jeunesse
dormitory	le dortoir
entrance hall	le vestibule
lounge	le salon
dining room	le restaurant
bedroom	une chambre
bath	le bain
shower	la douche
breakfast	le petit-déjeuner
lunch	le déjeuner
dinner	le dîner
meal	un repas
bill	l'addition
tip	un pourboire
service (included)	le service (compris)
waiter	le maître d'hôtel/le garçon
menu	la carte
wine (white and red)	le vin (blanc, rouge)
campsite	un terrain (de camping)
office	le bureau
warden	le gardien (le chef de camp)
caravan	la caravanne
tent	la tente
sanitary facilities	les sanitaires
washbasin	un lavabo
WC	WC
sink (for washing up)	un évier
sink (for clothes washing)	du linge
pitch	une place
electricity	l'électricité
water (drinkable)	l'eau (potable)
full	complet
open	ouvert
sleeping bag	sac de couchage
shady	ombragé
sunny	ensoleillé
quiet	tranquille

Shopping

shop	un magasin (une boutique)
supermarket	un supermarché
hypermarket	un hypermarché
market	le marché
butcher's shop	une boucherie
cooked meats shop	une charcuterie
bakery	une boulangerie
confectionery	une pâtisserie
general food	l'alimentation
stationery shop	une papeterie
bookseller	une librairie
chemist	une pharmacie
barber/hairdresser	un barbier (le coiffeur)
post office	le bureau de poste
tobacconist's shop	le bureau de tabac

Walking

help!	au secours!
map	la carte
rucksack	le sac à dos
compass	la boussole
mountain	une montagne
weather	le temps
snow	la neige
rain	la pluie
thunder	le tonnerre
fog	le brouillard
hot	chaud
cold	froid
peak	le sommet
shelter	un abri
rock	un rocher
cliff	la falaise
grass	l'herbe
footpath	un sentier
long-distance footpath	sentier de grande randonnée
signposted	balisé

open-air	en plein air
a walk	une promenade (une balade)
to walk	marcher (aller à pied)
hiking	le tourisme pédestre
short-cut	un raccourci
to climb	monter
forest	la forêt
I am lost	je suis perdu